My previous editor is getting married. I'm as happy as if it were happening to me!

–Tite Kubo

Bleach is author Tite Kubo's second title. Kubo made his debut with *ZOMBIEPOWDER.*, a four-volume series for *Weekly Shonen Jump*. To date, *Bleach* has been translated into numerous languages and has also inspired an animated TV series that began airing in the U.S. in 2006. Beginning its serialization in 2001, *Bleach* is still a mainstay in the pages of *Weekly Shonen Jump*. In 2005, *Bleach* was awarded the prestigious Shogakukan Manga Award in the *shonen* (boys) category.

BLEACH
VOL. 61: THE LAST 9 DAYS
SHONEN JUMP Manga Edition

STORY AND ART BY
TITE KUBO

Translation/Joe Yamazaki
Touch-up Art & Lettering/Mark McMurray
Design/Kam Li
Editor/Alexis Kirsch

BLEACH © 2001 by Tite Kubo. All rights reserved. First published in Japan in 2001 by SHUEISHA Inc., Tokyo. English translation rights arranged by SHUEISHA Inc.

The stories, characters and incidents mentioned in this publication are entirely fictional.

No portion of this book may be reproduced or transmitted in any form or by any means without written permission from the copyright holders.

Printed in the U.S.A.

Published by VIZ Media, LLC
P.O. Box 77010
San Francisco, CA 94107

10 9 8 7 6 5 4 3 2 1
First printing, August 2014

www.viz.com

I believe the world is full of danger

I want to protect you from it

Only because inside me is the same impulse as that danger

BLEACH 61 | THE LAST 9 DAYS

Shonen Jump Manga

ALL STARS ★ AND

Ichigo Kurosaki meets Soul Reaper Rukia Kuchiki and ends up helping her eradicate Hollows. After developing his powers as a Soul Reaper, Ichigo enters battle against Aizen and his dark ambitions! Ichigo finally defeats Aizen in exchange for his powers as a Soul Reaper.

With the battle over, Ichigo regains his normal life. But his tranquil days end when he meets Ginjo, who offers to help Ichigo get his powers back. But it was all a plot by Ginjo to steal Ichigo's new powers! Ginjo, who was the first ever Deputy Soul Reaper, then reveals to Ichigo the truth behind the deputy badge. However, even after learning the Soul Society's plans for him, Ichigo chooses to continue protecting his friends and defeats Ginjo.

Ichigo is sent back to the World of the Living by Squad Zero member Oh-Etsu Nimaiya, and there he learns about his past from Isshin. After finally learning the truth, Ichigo returns to Oh-Etsu and faces off against Zangetsu once again.

BLEACH

URYU ISHIDA

石田雨竜
イシダウリュウ

ユーハバッハ

YHWACH

HASCHWALTH

ハッシュヴァルト

STORIES

BLEACH 61

THE LAST 9DAYS

CONTENTS

541. THE BLADE AND ME 2 — 7
542. THE BLADE IS ME — 25
543. LETTERS — 43
544. WALKING WITH WATCHERS — 61
545. BLUE STRIPES — 79
546. THE LAST 9DAYS — 97
547. PEACE FROM SHADOWS — 115
548. THE THIN ICE — 137
549. THE STORMBRINGER — 155
550. BLAZING BULLETS — 173

541. THE BLADE AND ME 2

I TRIED NOT TO THINK ABOUT IT.

...WHEN I FIRST STOOD FACE TO FACE WITH HIM.

IT FELT LIKE I WAS DRAWN THERE.

I TRIED NOT TO THINK OF WHY THAT WAS.

...I THOUGHT HE WAS THE MOST IMPORTANT ENEMY.
WHY...

...STRAIGHT TO HIM WITHOUT KNOWING A THING.
WHY I WENT...

AND WHY...

...THE FIRST TIME I SAW HIM...

...HE ALMOST REMINDED ME OF SOMEBODY.

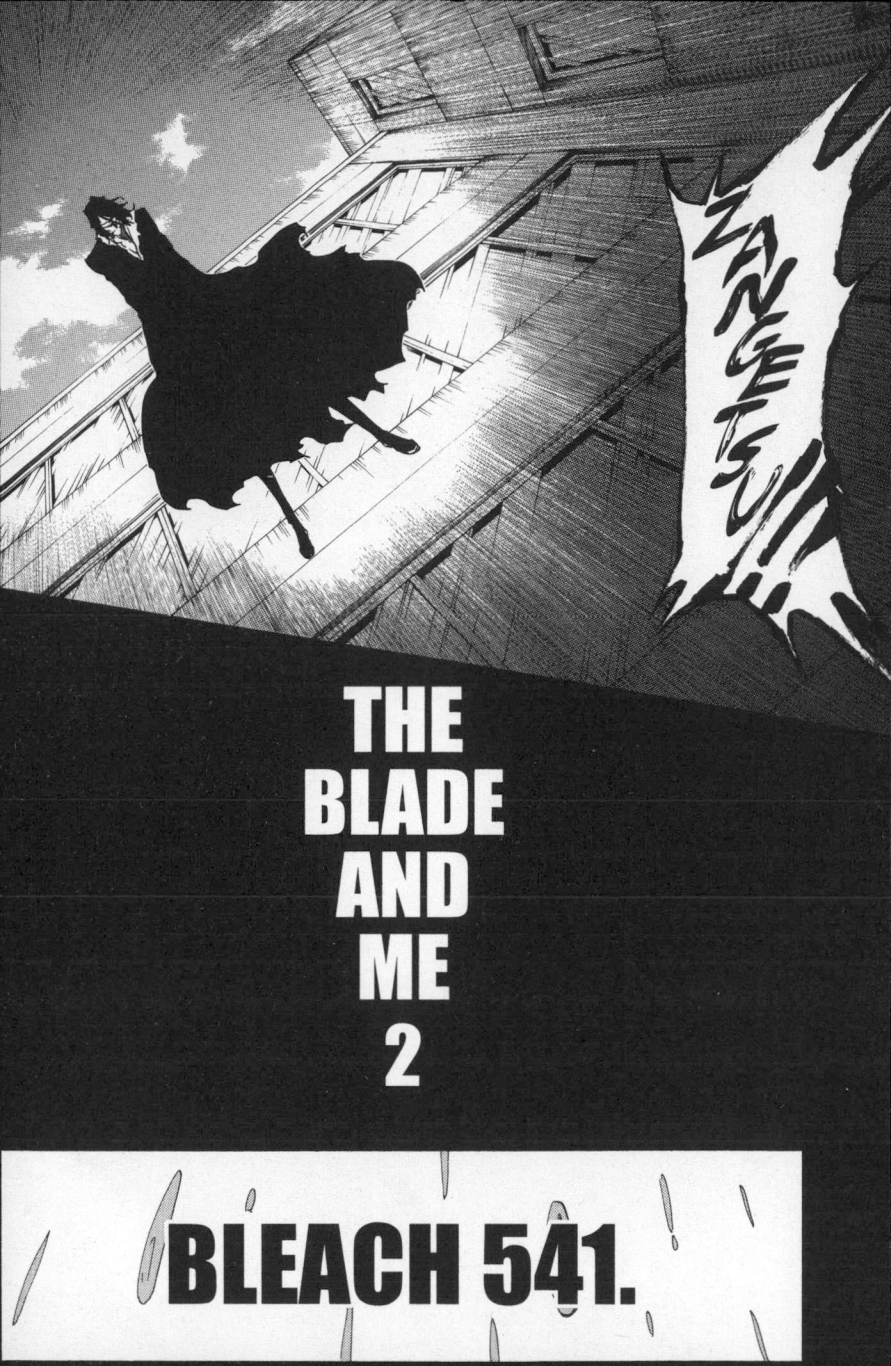
ZANGETSU!!
THE BLADE AND ME 2
BLEACH 541.

WHY...
...ZAN-GETSU ?
IT'S AS YOU WERE JUST TOLD.
AND...

I...
...AM NOT ZANGETSU.
GU
K
BO
OOSH

ARE YOU REALLY...
...NOT ZAN-GETSU ?
ARE YOU REALLY...
... YHWACH ?
I AM...
...THE SOURCE OF THE QUINCY POWER INSIDE YOU.
I AM YHWACH AND I AM NOT YHWACH.
I DON'T UNDER-STAND !!
ARE YOU MY ENEMY ?!
OR ARE YOU MY FRIEND ?!
WAS EVERY-THING YOU SAID TO ME A LIE ?!

WHICH IS IT ?!!

EXCEPT FOR THE NAME I TOLD YOU.
I AM NOT YOUR ENEMY ...
OR YOUR FRIEND.
BUT ...
...THERE ARE NO LIES IN MY WORDS OR MY HEART.
ICHI-GO...
I KNOW YOU'VE SEEN IT.

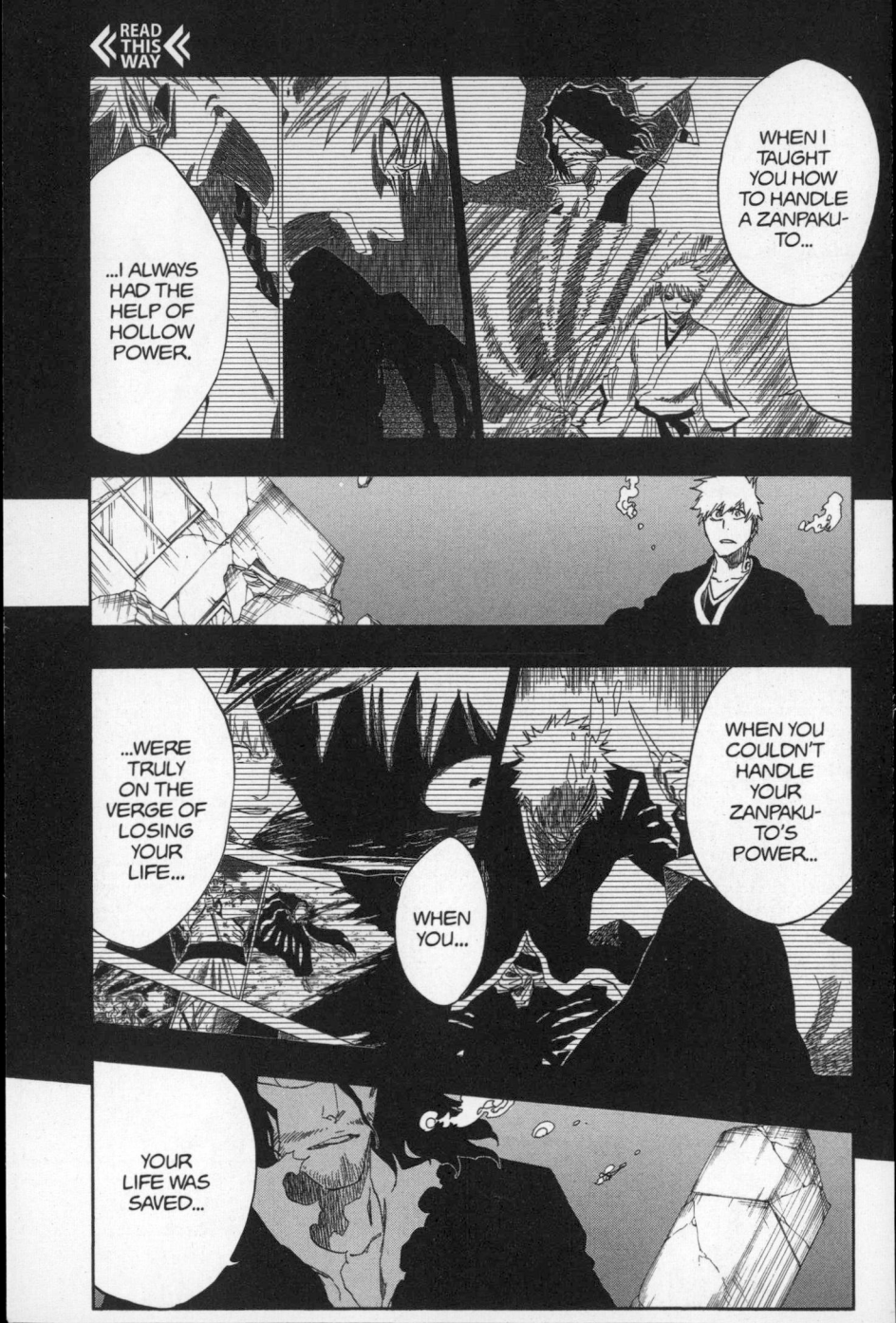
READ THIS WAY
WHEN I TAUGHT YOU HOW TO HANDLE A ZANPAKU-TO...
...I ALWAYS HAD THE HELP OF HOLLOW POWER.
WHEN YOU COULDN'T HANDLE YOUR ZANPAKU-TO'S POWER...
...WERE TRULY ON THE VERGE OF LOSING YOUR LIFE...
WHEN YOU...
YOUR LIFE WAS SAVED...

BUT BY A HOLLOW.
...NOT BY ME.
THAT IS WHY...
...I SUPPRESSED YOUR POWER THAT WAS STILL NOT YET MATURE...
...AND PERSONALLY BECAME THE CENTER OF YOUR POWER.
I...
...DID NOT WANT YOU TO BE A SOUL REAPER.

WHAT IS THERE TO QUESTION ...
...ABOUT WANTING TO KEEP YOU FAR AWAY FROM DANGER, FROM CONFLICT?
"WHY"?
...
WHY...?
YOU WOULD SUFFER.
YOU WOULD BE HURT.
...YOU WOULD HAVE BEEN DRAGGED INTO BATTLE WHETHER YOU WANTED TO OR NOT.
IF YOU HAD BECOME A SOUL REAPER..
...I WOULD HAVE TO KILL YOU MYSELF.
AND EVENTUALLY ...
FWAP

BOOF
GRIP
WOOSH
IF YOU BECAME ONE, I WOULD HAVE TO KILL YOU.
I COULD NOT LET YOU BE A SOUL REAPER.

THAT IS WHAT I THOUGHT ...

HOW-EVER ...
...YOU CHOSE THE PATH OF A SOUL REAPER.
YOU WERE GIVEN AN OPPOR-TUNITY.
YOU STRENGTH-ENED YOUR-SELF.
THROUGH PAIN AND SUFFER-ING...
...YOU TRAVELED DOWN THAT PATH WITH YOUR OWN FREE WILL.

AS I WATCHED YOU...
...I COULD ALMOST HEAR MY HEART WAVERING.
EVEN-TUALLY ...
...MY WISH OF KEEPING YOU FAR AWAY FROM SOUL REAPERS...
...TILTED TOWARD HELPING YOUR DECISION.
AND...
...NOW I...

ZSSH

...IN STEPPING AWAY.

...ALMOST FEEL JOY...

READ THIS WAY
I STILL HAVEN'T ...
W...
WAIT, ZANGETSU !!

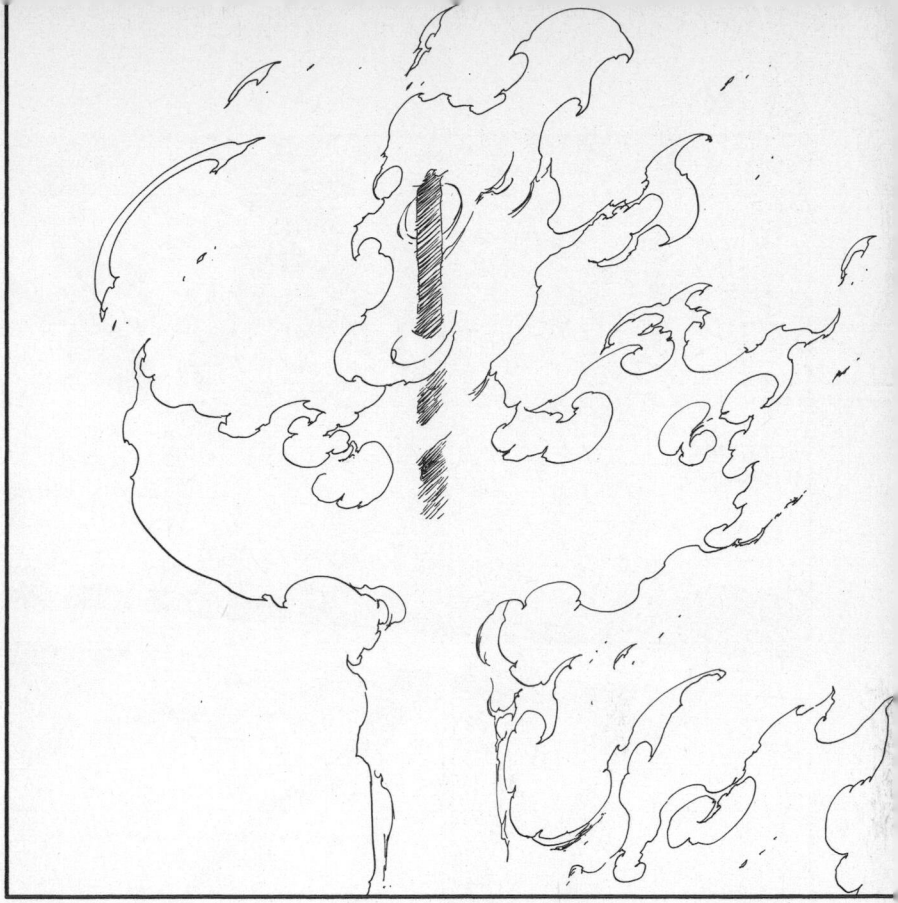

TAKE IT.
THAT IS YOUR TRUE ZANPAKU-TO...
...FIGHT WITH YOUR OWN POWER.
YOU CAN NOW...
ICHI-GO.
...IS MERELY A FRAGMENT OF YOUR POWER THAT I COULD NOT CONTAIN.
WHAT YOU'VE BEEN USING ...

THAT IS ZANGETSU.

542. THE BLADE IS ME

ZANGETSU.

I DON'T CARE WHO YOU ARE.

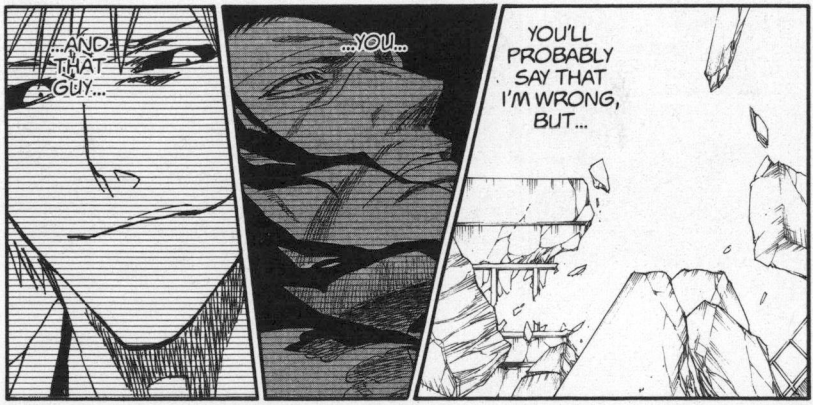
...AND THAT GUY...
...YOU...
YOU'LL PROBABLY SAY THAT I'M WRONG, BUT...

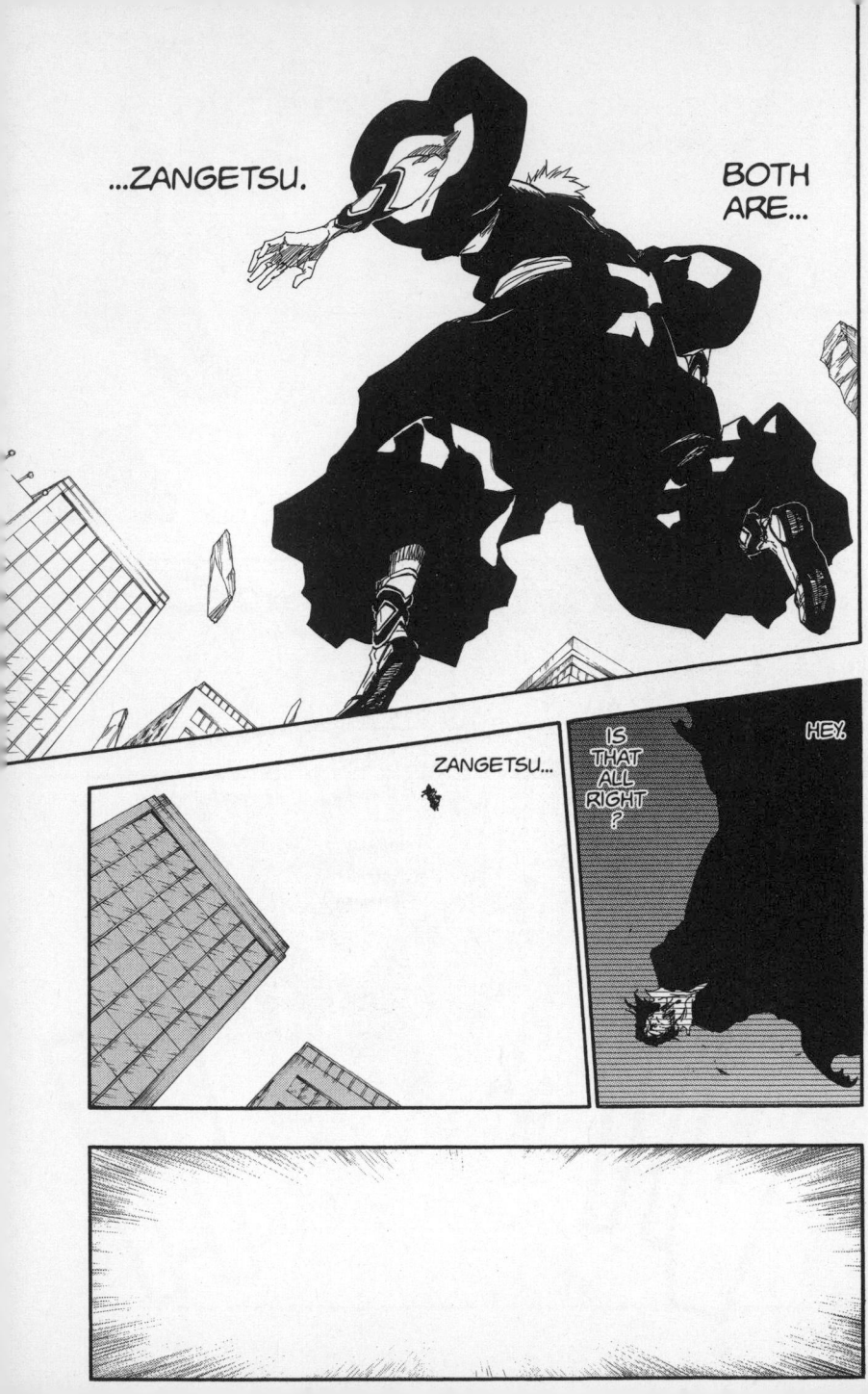
...ZANGETSU.
BOTH ARE...
ZANGETSU...
IS THAT ALL RIGHT?
HEY.

GWOOOF

NO
OSE!

YOUR HANDS...
A...
ARE YOU CRAZY?!
IT'S ALL GOOD.
RIGHT, GO-ICHI?

I WAS JUST THINKING...
...IT'D BE...
...COMPLETE ONCE...
...YOUR SOUL'S...
...BEEN PUT INTO IT.

GO ON.
PULL IT OUT, GO-ICHI!

THAT...
...IS YOUR ZANPAKU-TO!

GRP...

BOOM
SH

WOOSH
WOOOOOOOO...

HELL NO!
HAVE YOU EVER SEEN ANY-THING LIKE THIS ...?

THE WATER'S GONE...!
...

IN ORDER TO COOL THE SOUL OF THE SWORD.
THE SEA DRIED UP FROM THE HEAT AND SPIRITUAL PRESSURE.

YOU THINK YOU CAN GET ALONG?
WHAT D'YOU THINK, GO-ICHI?

WITH...

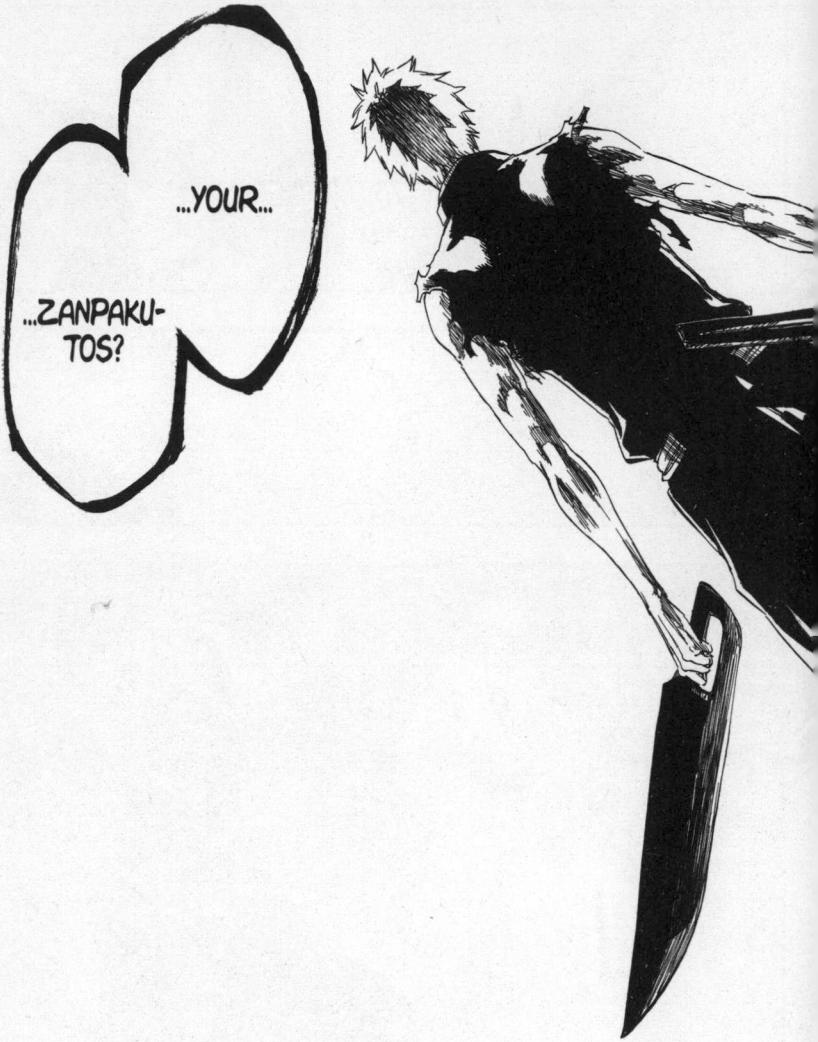
...YOUR...
...ZANPAKU-TOS?

GCHK…

...WILL FIGHT ON MY OWN.

I...

BLEACH 542.

...ME.

YOU ARE...

THE BLADE

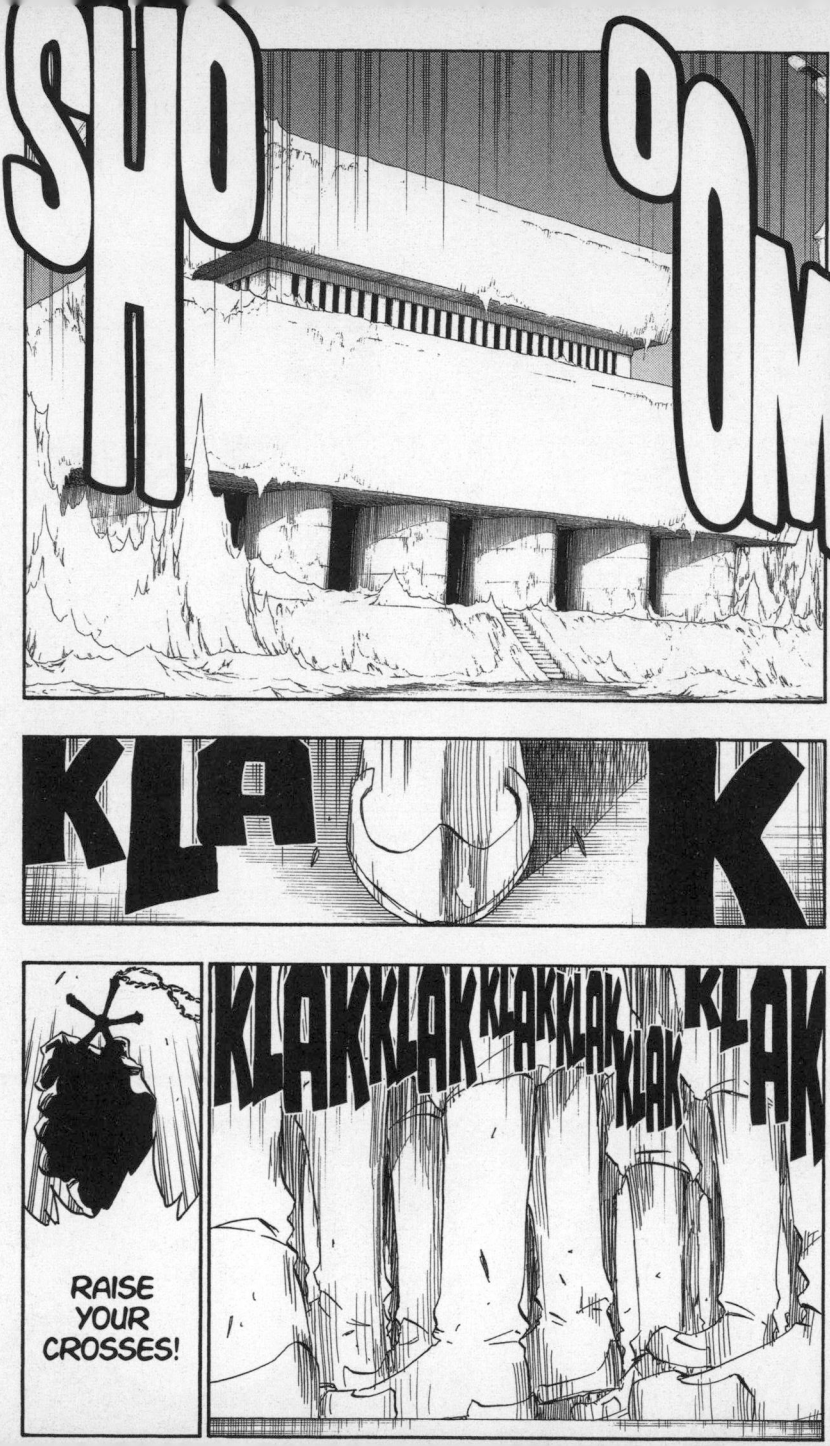
SHOOM
KLAK
RAISE YOUR CROSSES!
KLAKKLAKKLAKKLAKKLAKKLAK

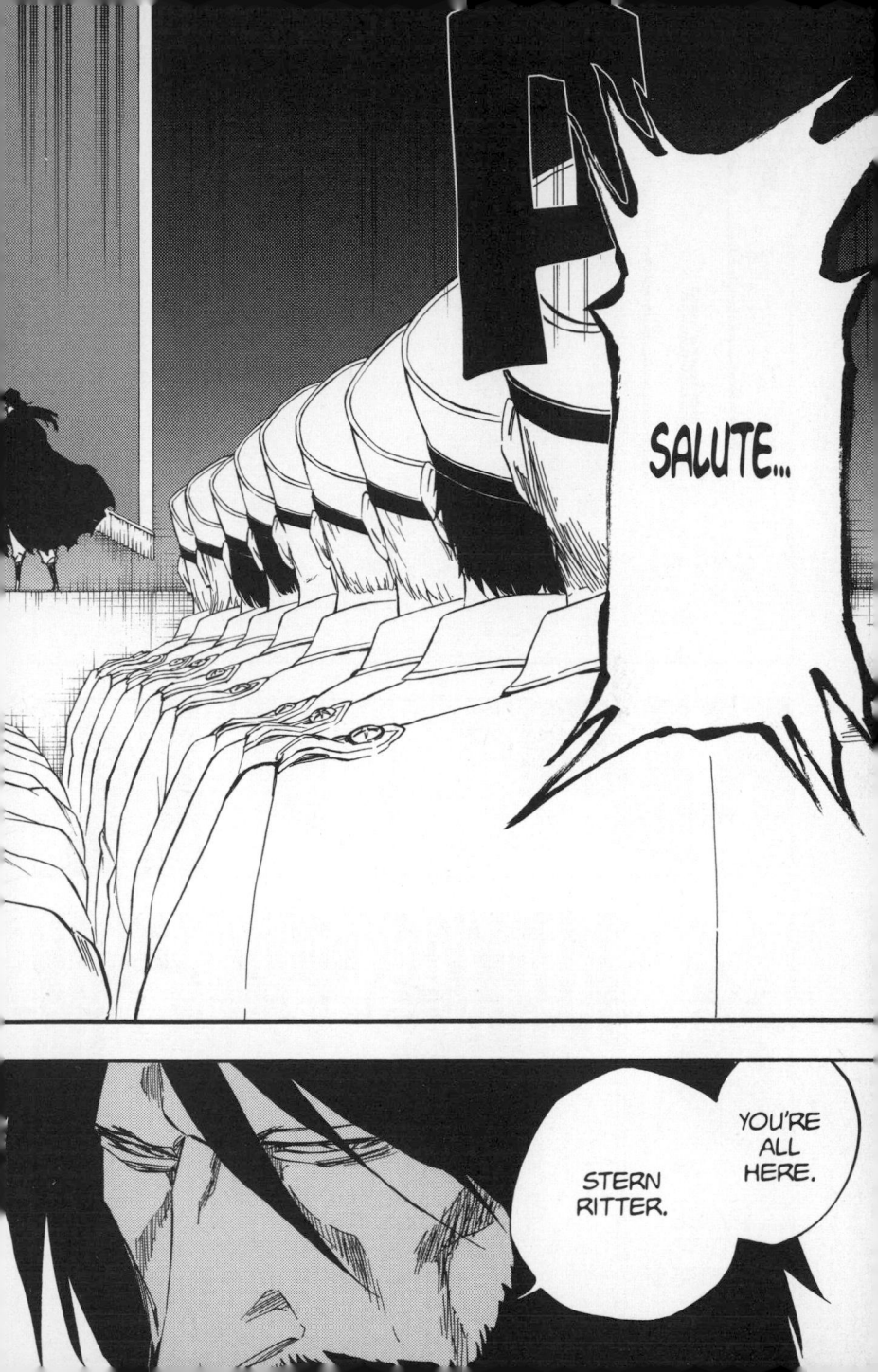
SALUTE...
YOU'RE ALL HERE.
STERN RITTER.

...HIS MAJESTY YHWACH!!
...NEWS TO SHARE WITH YOU.
I HAVE SOME...

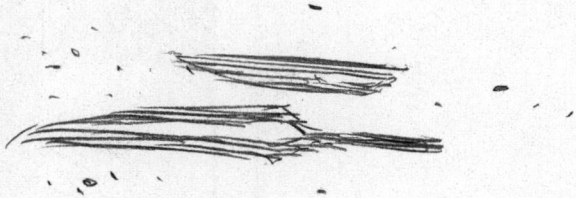

STERN RITTER.
I HAVE SOME NEWS TO SHARE WITH YOU.
COME.
TMP

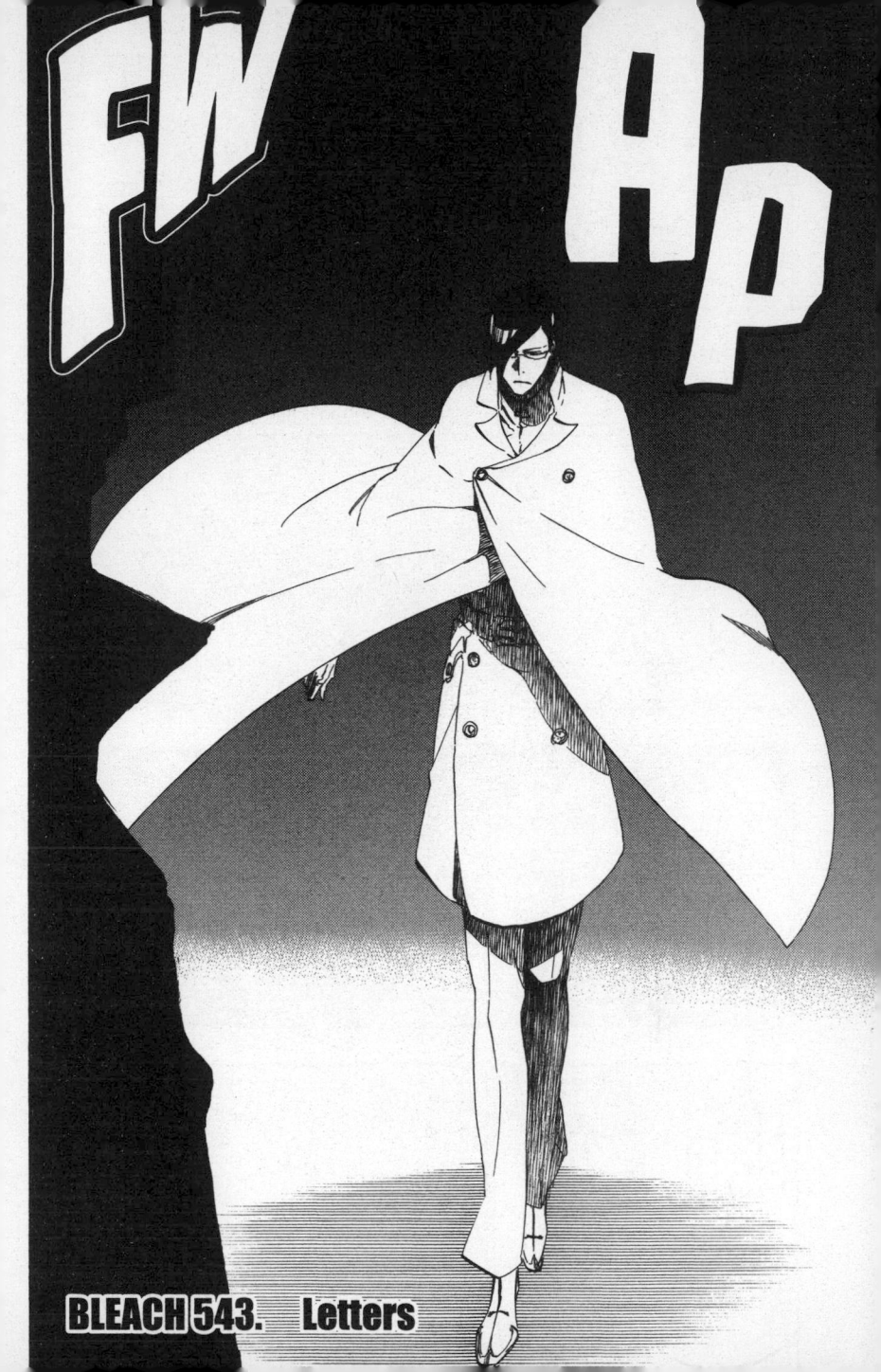

BLEACH 543. Letters

GASP
WHAT ...?

MUTT...ER
MUTTER
MUTTER
WHY IS HE ON THE SAME STAGE AS HIS MAJESTY ...?
WHO IS THAT GUY...?!
MUTTER

URYU ISHIDA.
HE IS THE LAST SURVIVING QUINCY IN THIS WORLD.

I AM...

...APPOINT-
ING HIM...

...AS MY SUCCESSOR.

WHAT DID HIS MAJESTY JUST SAY ...?
WHAT ...?

WHY ...?
SOME GUY WE DON'T EVEN KNOW ...?!
HIS MAJESTY'S SUCCESSOR ...?!

STAMP

!
FWP
HOLD ON A SECOND, YOUR MAJESTY !!

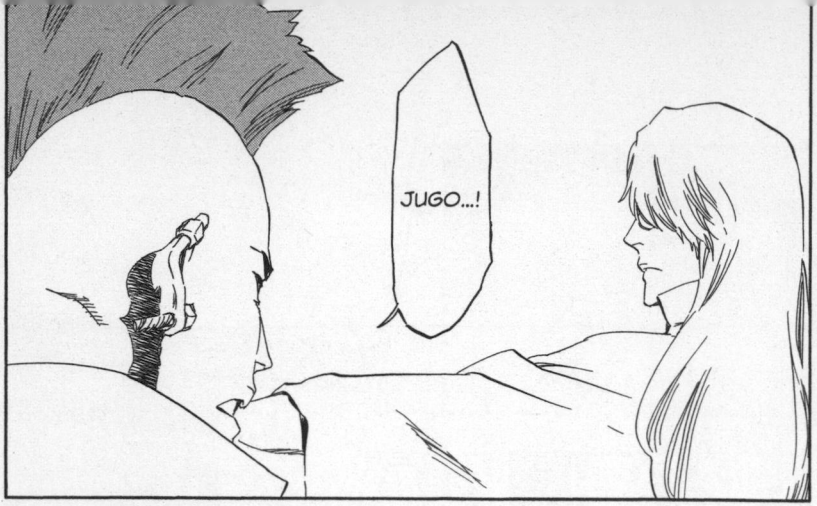
JUGO...!

YOU ALL WILL SOON LEARN FIRSTHAND...
NO NEED FOR CONCERN EITHER.
I WILL NOT STAND FOR OBJEC-TIONS.

...HIS POWER IN THE BATTLES TO COME.

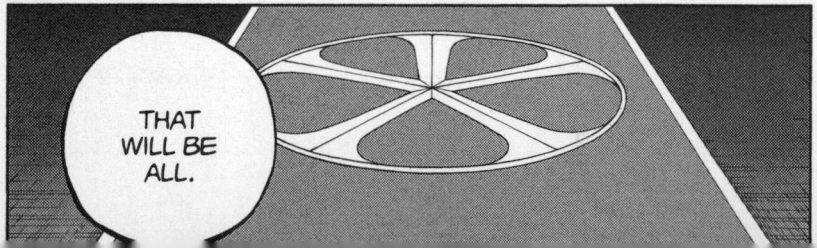
THAT WILL BE ALL.

POP
KRAK
KRAK
WHAT THE HELL WAS THAT ?!
WHO IS THAT GUY?!
WILL SOME-BODY PLEASE EXPLAIN IT TO ME!!
I DON'T UNDER-STAND IT AT ALL!!

Stern Ritter
"S"
Mask De Masculine
AN EXPLANATION...?
Stern Ritter
"K"
BG9
ONLY HIS MAJESTY COULD ANSWER THOSE QUESTIONS...
...
Stern Ritter
"I"
Cang Du
I AIN'T ACCEPTING IT...
Stern Ritter
"H"
Bazz-B
DAMN IT!

KRSK
GET OUTTA MY WAY!
I SAID NOT NOW!
SHOOP
H-HEY!
WHERE YOU GOING, BAZZ-B ?!
TO HIS MAJESTY'S!
I'M GONNA GO TALK TO HIM!
WHA ...
STOP!
YOU THINK HIS MAJESTY WILL TOLERATE THAT?!
BAZZ-B!!
TMP
!

READ THIS WAY
TMp...
JUGO ...
Stern Ritter
"B"
Jugram Haschwalth

WHAT ABOUT YOU? SHOULDN'T YOU BE GOING SOME-WHERE TOO?
WHERE ARE YOU GOING, BAZZ-B ...?
YOU KNOW ...
I WAS UNDER THE IMPRESSION THAT YOU WERE HIS MAJESTY'S SUCCES-SOR.
MOST OF THE RITTERS WOULD HAVE NO COMPLAINTS IF YOU WERE THE CHOICE.
AND YET YOU HAVE NO PROBLEM WITH THIS?!
HIS MAJESTY HAS MADE HIS DECISION.
THERE IS NO ROOM FOR ME TO QUESTION IT.
TCH...
YOU'VE BECOME A COWARD.
WHAT A LET-DOWN.
TMP...

THEN GIVE UP YOUR SEAT RIGHT NOW!!
IF YOU'RE JUST GONNA GIVE IT UP TO THAT NOBODY ...
...I'LL TAKE IT FROM YOU!!
HUH ?!
I AM CALM!
A LOT MORE THAN YOU ARE RIGHT NOW!!
CALM DOWN, BAZZ-B.

DROP

!!

YOU'RE RIGHT ...
YOU ARE CALM.

NAKK LE VAAR...
WHAT DO YOU THINK YOU'RE DOING...?
HELPING YOU.
FIGHTING IS NO GOOD.
HIS MAJESTY DOESN'T LIKE CONFLICT AND...
...YOU HAVE EYES ON YOU.
CLAP
YOU'RE CALM.
YOU DIDN'T CHARGE HEAD-FIRST.
VERY CALM...
CLAP
CLAP...
Stern Ritter "D"
Askin Nakk Le Vaar
GEH!
GEH!
GEH!

I KNOW YOU ALREADY KNOW THAT.
DON'T YOU?
ESPE-CIALLY FOR YOU.
IT'LL ONLY BE POISON.
NOTHING GOOD'LL COME OF IT.
CUT IT OUT.
THE BOTH OF YOU.
OUR NEXT EMPEROR.
WHOOOSH

YOU SHALL RECEIVE ...

...THE SAME LETTER "A" AS ME.

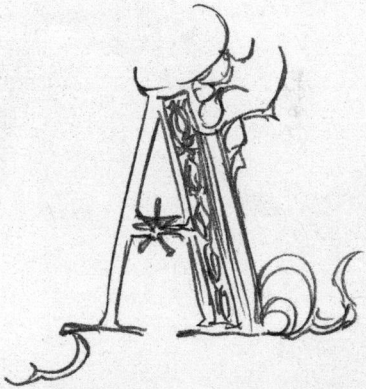

544. WALKING WITH WATCHERS

URYU.

WHY ARE YOU...

...STILL ALIVE?

IT SEEMS YOU PICK THINGS UP QUICKLY.
!
NINE YEARS AGO ...
...EVERY GEMISCHTE (MIXED-BLOOD) QUINCY PERISHED UNDER...
...THE AUSWÄHLEN I CONDUCTED.
EXCEPT FOR YOU.
YOU ...
...ARE THE ONLY QUINCY EVER TO SURVIVE THE CONSE-CRATION .
...REFERRED TO YOU AS THE LAST SURVIVOR.
THAT IS WHY I...

YOU...
...HAVE SOME KIND OF POWER THAT EXCEEDS MY OWN.

THAT IS...
...THE REASON WHY YOU ARE THE SUCCESSOR.

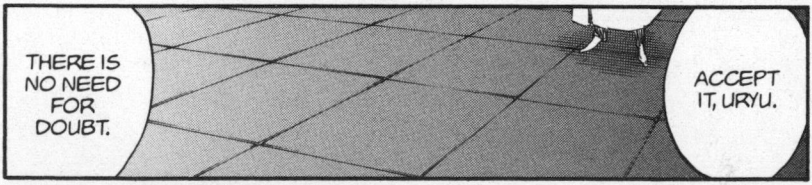
ACCEPT IT, URYU.
THERE IS NO NEED FOR DOUBT.

COME WITH ME.

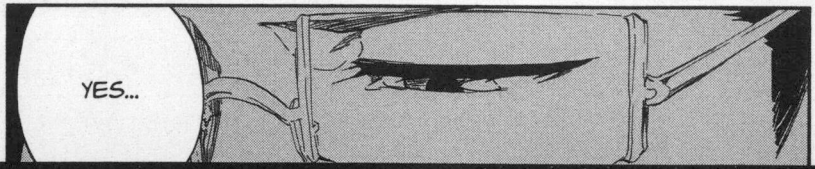

I UNDER-STAND...

...YOUR MAJESTY...

BLEACH 544.

Walking With Watchers

YES, MA'AM!

M-ME ?!
YUP. YOU!
COME TO MY ROOM. I NEED RELIEF.
RIGHT THIS SEC-OND!
FWUSH
IT--
IT'S AN HONOR !!

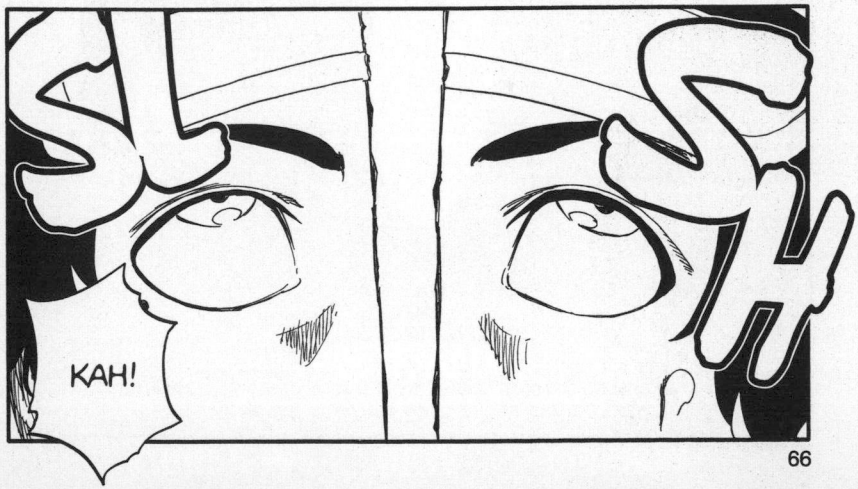
SLASH
KAH!

PLOP
PLOP
PLOP
PAAAAA...
SPLAAAT
LOOK AT THE MESS YOU MADE AGAIN !!
AW, C'MON.
KCHK
TMP TMPTMP

YOU GUYS MAKE A LOT OF MESSES TOO.

I JUST THINK YOU COULD AT LEAST DO IT OUTSIDE...
Stern Ritter "P"
Meninas McAllon
YOU STUPID BITCH.
COOKIE CRUMBS AND BLOOD SPLATTER ARE NOT THE SAME.
Stern Ritter "G"
Liltotto-Lamperd
CUZ YOU LIKE PICKING UP HOT SUB-ORDINATES, DON'T YOU, CANDY?
Stern Ritter "Z"
Giselle Gewelle
THE PROBLEM IS HER KILLING HOT GUYS WHENEVER SHE'S PISSED!
IT'S NOT ABOUT INSIDE OR OUT-SIDE!
Stern Ritter "T"
Candice Catnipp

GLUNK
YOU PICKING A FIGHT WITH ME, GIGI?!
LOOK AT ME !!
HUH ?!
THAT'S NOT WHAT I'M SAYING!
WHAT'S BOTHERING YOU?
WHAT ...?
I GOT A LOT ON MY MIND RIGHT NOW.
YOU MIND KEEPING IT DOWN...?
K...R E... E...

READ THIS WAY
WHAT DO YOU THINK?
I'M WORRIED ABOUT THE FUTURE OF THE VANDEN-REICH.
KCHAK...
WEL-COME BACK...
MASTER HASCH-WALTH.

YOU'RE STILL UP?

IT'S LATE.
GET SOME REST.

I HEARD ABOUT IT.
HIS MAJESTY'S ANNOUNCE-MENT.

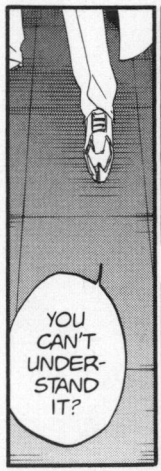
YOU CAN'T UNDER-STAND IT?

YOU DON'T APPROVE ?

DO YOU, MASTER HASCH-WALTH?

IT MAY NOT BE MY PLACE TO SAY.
BUT I...
...BE-LIEVE HIS MAJESTY COULD USE YOUR COUNSEL.

HIS MAJESTY IS WELL AWARE OF THAT.
NAMING HIS SUCCESSOR IN THAT MANNER WILL BREED UNREST WITHIN THE RITTER.
IT IS...
...HIS MAJESTY'S WISH.
...HIS MAJESTY'S INTENTION TO CAUSE UNREST.
IT WAS...
THEN THERE IS ONLY ONE ANSWER.
NO MATTER WHO HE IS...
NO MATTER WHAT KIND OF POWER HE POSSESSES ...
NO MATTER WHAT HE'S UP TO...
HE NOW ...
...WILL BE DIRECTED AT URYU ISHIDA.
UNREST CAUSES SCRUTINY IN THE RANKS.
MORE SO...
...ALL OF THAT SCRUTINY...

...CANNOT MAKE THE SLIGHTEST MOVE.

HIS ONLY...
...PATH NOW IS TO DEDICATE HIMSELF...
...TO HIS MAJESTY'S WILL.

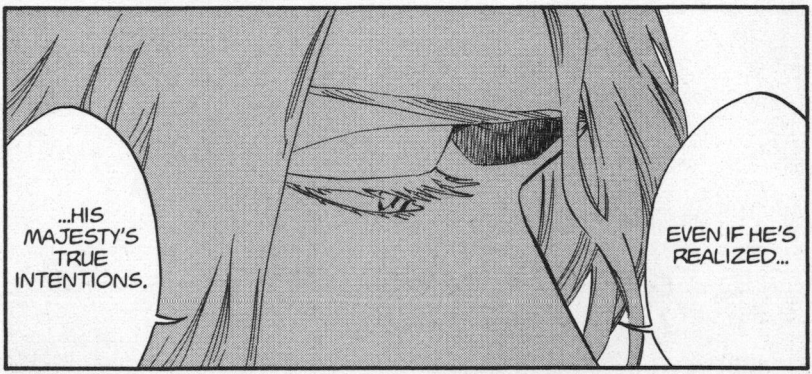
EVEN IF HE'S REALIZED...
...HIS MAJESTY'S TRUE INTENTIONS.

FLOP
I'M FINALLY HERE!!
PHAAA!
THUD

I KNOW TRAVELING'S A PART OF TRAINING, BUT THIS NEGAL RUIN WAS SO FAR AWAY...
RUSTL RUSTL

YOU MUST BE TIRED TOO, PERO!
WHAT'S IT MADE FROM ANYWAYS...? I'M SCARED...
YUCK... WHAT IS THIS...?
HE WAS SO CONCERNED WITH WHAT THIS DELICIOUS POTATO-LIKE THING WAS MADE FROM. I WONDER IF HE GOT HERE ALL RIGHT...?
CHEW CHEW CHEW
WONDER HOW CHAD IS DOING...
KRSH

I'LL HAVE HIM GO WITH YOU JUST TO BE SAFE!
HE'S EQUIPPED WITH A CAMERA, SO DON'T WORRY!
I'LL BE RIGHT THERE IF ANYTHING HAPPENS!
NO.
NOT AT ALL PERO!

CHAD!
GOOD, YOU GOT HERE BEFORE ME...
!
ZSH
TOOK YOU LONG ENOUGH, INOUE!
...HE DIDN'T COME WHEN I WAS IN DAN-GER.
RMBL RMBL RMBL
WHY WOULD HE SAY THAT...?
IS WHAT HE SAID, BUT...

EVERY-BODY'S HERE!

EVERY-BODY ...?
WAIT?
WHAT ...?!

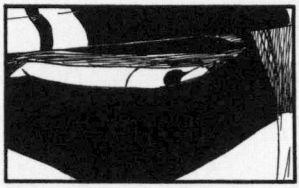

SO SHE GOT HERE SAFELY...
GOOD ...

LOOKS LIKE...
GRK...
...THIS IS GOING TO TAKE SOME MORE TIME.
GRKL...

KUROSAKI CLINIC

Love You
Berry Much

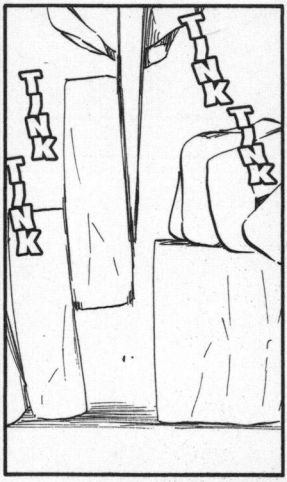
TINK
TINK
TINK
TINK

SHAAAA

TIME TO EAT!
DAD! KARIN!

I'LL BE DOWN AFTER I KILL THIS BOSS!!
HOLD ON!
OKEY-DOKEY! LET ME GET RID OF THIS PATIENT AND I'LL BE RIGHT THERE!!
HEY! ARE YOU TALKING ABOUT ME, DOC?!
重症

I KNOW!
NO MORE AFTER THAT, OKAY?!

I WISH ...
...ICHIGO WAS BACK FROM TRAINING CAMP.

545.
Blue Stripes

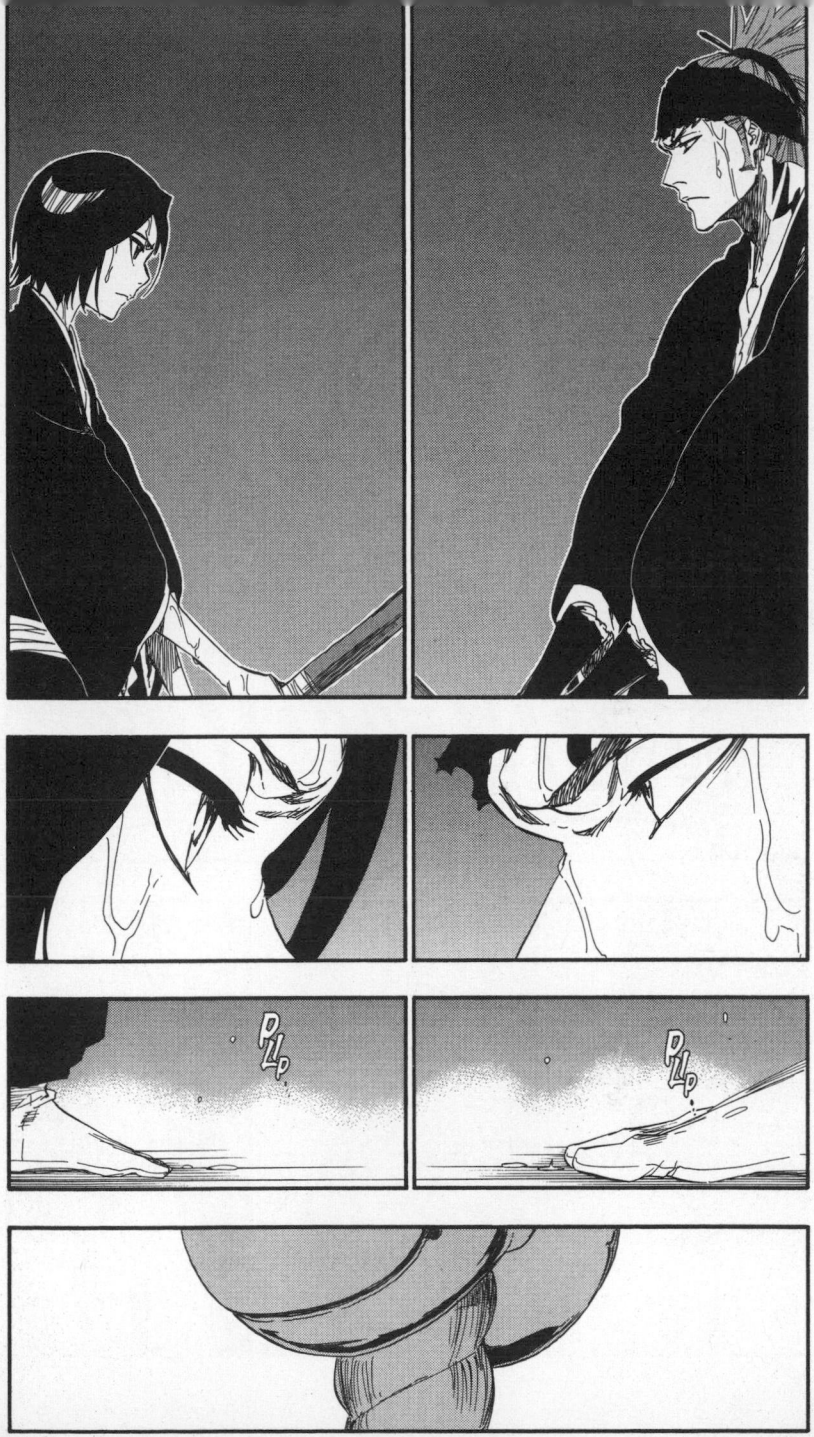
PLP.
PLP.

CLANG CLANG CLANG CLANG
PHAAAAAAA!!

WHAT'S SO TOUGH ABOUT STANDING STILL AND FACING EACH OTHER!
SHUT UP!
YOU SHUT UP. IT'S NOT FOR ME!
STANDING STILL OR POINTING A SWORD AT A FRIEND!

HUWEE !!
DAMN, THAT'S TOUGH !!
THUD

I-I DON'T LIKE POINTING MY SWORD AT FRIENDS EITHER!
SEE, YOU'RE EXHAUSTED TOO.

PLUS ...
...WE'RE STILL NOT USED TO THE AIR HERE.

TRUE.
THE REISHI DENSITY OF THE ATMOSPHERE HERE IS INCREDIBLE.

BEEP BEEP BEEP
!

IT DOESN'T FEEL COMPLETELY OVERWHELMING NOW...
BUT IT STILL FEELS LIKE BEING UNDERWATER.
I HAVE NO IDEA WHAT EFFECT THIS KIND OF REISHI DENSITY HAS ON US...

THE GREASER FROM THE HOT SPRING.
WHAT'S UP WITH NOT SHOWING MY FACE IN A FLASHBACK?
OH.
THAT WAS KIRINJI!
WHEN DID YOU GUYS EXCHANGE NUMBERS ...?

?
WHO IS IT ?
YES!
YES!
YES, THIS IS KUCHIKI!
YES ...
REALLY ?!

...HEALED!
MY BROTHER'S ...

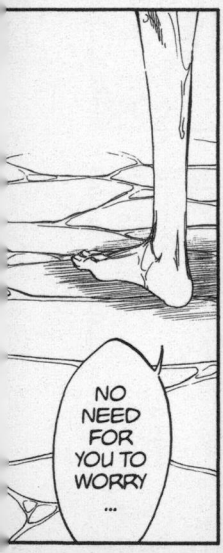
NO NEED FOR YOU TO WORRY ...

YOU LIGHT-HEADED AT ALL?
WELL ?

麒麟殿
THAT WAS A LONG BATH...
YOU'RE THE FIRST TO BATHE THIS LONG IN MY HOT SPRING.

I'M AWARE...
...THAT MY POWER IS STILL NOT DEVELOPED ENOUGH FOR ME TO GET LIGHT-HEADED.
HAVING SURVIVED ...
...I NOW NEED TO GAIN A POWER DESERVING OF FEELING LIGHT-HEADED.
HE'S HEALED ?!
GREAT!
WAIT, THAT MEANS HE'LL EAT, TRAIN HIS SWORD, THEN...
YUP, THEN GO THERE ...

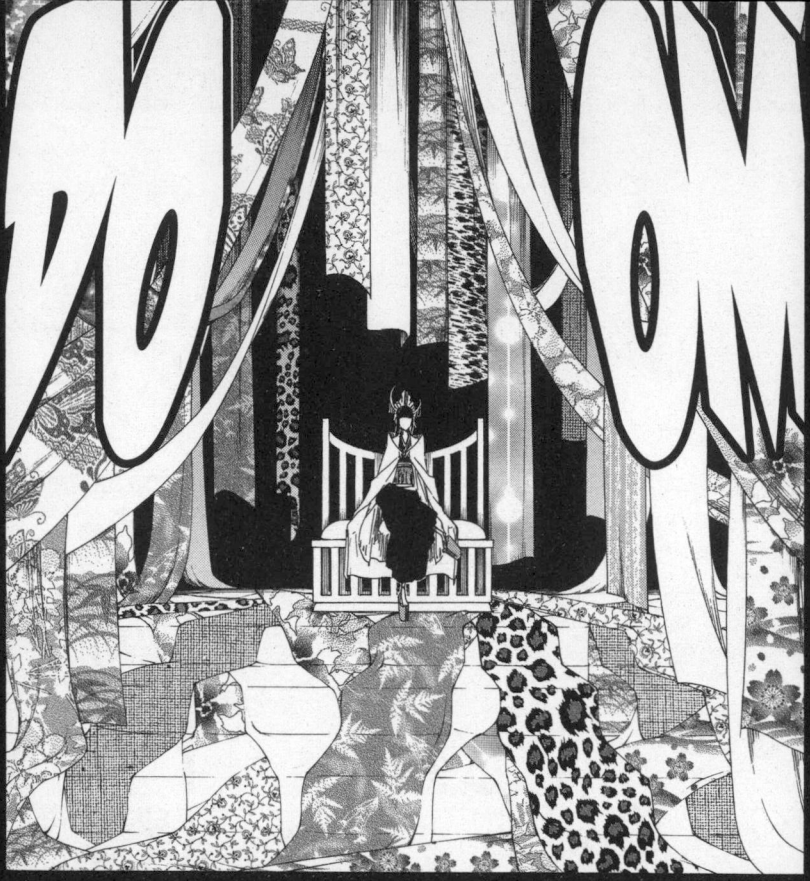
BOOM

THAT PLACE WAS AWFUL ...
A MEASUREMENT FROM HELL...
YEAH ...
STRIPPED NAKED...
I DON'T EVEN WANT TO THINK ABOUT IT...
HEY! REN-JI!
NO! DON'T DO IT!
REN-JI!!
WHY ARE YOU TRYING TO REMEMBER IT?!
BORK
BORK
BORK

HUH?

WAIT, WAIT.
WHY CAN'T WE DO THAT WITH MY LOIN-CLOTH ON?
WE'RE TAKING MEASURE-MENTS FOR A SHI-HAKUSHO, RIGHT?
I SAID TAKE OFF YOUR LOIN-CLOTH TOO.
DO NOT RESPOND WITH A QUESTION.
YOU HEARD WHAT I SAID.
I SEE ...
I'LL TAKE MEASURE-MENTS AFTER I REMOVE YOUR JEWELS.
ALL RIGHT.
I UNDER-STAND.
OKAY! I'M TAKING IT OFF RIGHT NOW!!!
BUT ...
...MORE IMPORTANTLY, TO THINK MY BROTHER HAS TO GO THROUGH THE SAME HUMILIATION...
POOR BYAKUYA ...
MORE IMPOR-TANTLY ...?
GASP
HMMM...
YOU BACK, RENJI ?!
GOOD!
I'M GLAD YOU DIDN'T REACH THE PART WHERE YOU TOOK IT OFF!!

UWAHAHAHAHAH!!

GOOD TO SEE YOU GUYS TALKING!
SQUAD ZERO "MANAKO OSHO" (HIGH PRIEST)
ICHIBE HYOSUBE

SO?
IS IT TIME TO TRAIN WITH ME INSIDE?
THIS IS QUITE AN IMPROVEMENT. WELL DONE!
WHEN YOU FIRST GOT HERE, THE REISHI WAS SO THICK YOU TWO COULD BARELY MOVE OR BREATHE.
FWP
YES, SIR !!!
五
LIKE I SAID!

I CAN TELL EVEN OVER THE PHONE THAT YOU'RE NOT BOWING YOUR HEAD!!!
HEAD DOWN? YEAH RIGHT !!
I'M BEGGING FOR YOUR HELP, WITH MY HEAD DOWN!!
THIS ISN'T AN ORDER!!
THAT WAS FAST !!
THERE'S A PACKAGE FROM THE SOUL SOCIETY.
THEY ACTUALLY HAVE A POSTAL SERVICE ?!
DON'T HANG UP, DAMN IT!!
HEY ?!
LOOK, I'M COUNTING ON YOU, OKAY ?!
YOU'RE THE ONLY ONE WHO CAN DO IT!!
HOW DO YOU LIKE THAT CHOSEN-ONE FEELING?! PRETTY GOOD, HUH?! LATER!!
BZZZ
HIYORI.
...MAYURI KUROTSUCHI.
SHINJI HIRAKO AND...
IT WAS SENT FROM TWO PEOPLE.

FIXING THE SUPER PAIN-IN-THE-BUTT DISTORTION BETWEEN THE WORLD OF THE LIVING AND THE SOUL SOCIETY CREW...
AW, DAMN IT! ALL RIGHT, I'LL FREAKIN' DO IT!!!
...HAS BEEN FORMED !!

OF COURSE !!!
WE'RE A PART OF IT?
FORMED ...?

ICHIGO?

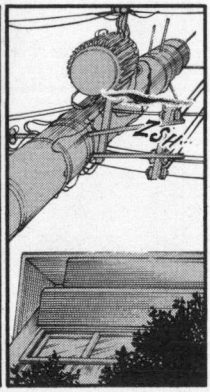
ZSH!!

I'M ALL OUT OF OPTIONS NOW.
SO YOU DON'T EITHER ...?
HOW THE HELL SHOULD I KNOW?

I JUST THOUGHT YOU MIGHT KNOW WHERE HE WAS.
WELL...

...CHAD AND INOUE AND ISHIDA ARE ALSO GONE, SO IT'S PROBABLY SOMETHING THAT HAS TO DO WITH THE SOUL SOCIETY.
EITHER WAY...
THAT BAS-TARD ...

THEY SAID HE WAS PRACTICING WITH THE SOCCER TEAM.
AL-THOUGH THE TOUR-NAMENT ENDED LAST MONTH.
DID YOU ASK YUZU OR KARIN?

I'M SURE THEY'LL BE BACK ONE OF THESE DAYS.

TMP...
PARDON ME...

WHO THE...?
YOU IDIOT! HE OBVIOUSLY HAS SOMETHING TO DO WITH ICHIGO!

YOU'RE THE CAPTAIN OF SQUAD EIGHT, AREN'T YOU?
I RECALL AN OFFICER CALLING YOU THAT DURING THE AFTERMATH OF THE AIZEN BATTLE.
TMP

READ THIS WAY
SEEING THAT A CAPTAIN IS HERE MUST MEAN IT'S SOMETHING IMPORTANT.
HOW CAN WE HELP YOU?
ALTHOUGH I WOULD BE EVEN MORE SO IF YOU WERE A GIRL.
I'M ECSTATIC YOU REMEMBER ME.
...I NEED TO TELL YOU ALL.
THERE'S SOME-THING...
YEAH ...
...SAYING GOODBYE TO ICHIGO.
IT'S ABOUT...

SOCCER PRACTICE, EH...?
GAME

WH...

WHOA, WHOA, WHOA, WHOA, WHOA ...

YOU'RE NOT JOKING, YET YOU'RE TELLING US TO SAY GOODBYE JUST LIKE THAT?

KEIGO, STOP...
YOU GUYS PROBABLY GOT HIM MIXED UP IN SOME-THING AGAIN, DIDN'T YOU?!
AS IF IT'S GOT NOTHING TO DO WITH YOU...

JUST AS YOU SUS-PECT.
...THE SOUL SOCIETY RIGHT NOW TO PROTECT IT.
ICHI-GO IS IN...
THAT'S EXACTLY RIGHT...

...WHY DOES THAT HAVE TO MEAN SAYING GOODBYE TO HIM?
BUT...
THAT'S FINE...
THAT'S WHO HE IS.
THAT'S WHY WE'RE FRIENDS WITH HIM.

WHAT I'M WOR-RIED ABOUT IS...
ALTHOUGH...
...KNOWING HIM, I'M SURE HE'LL COME BACK SAFELY.
THE PLACE HE'S IN NOW IS A VERY SPECIAL PLACE EVEN WITHIN THE SOUL SOCIETY.

...WHAT KIND OF POWER HE'LL COME BACK WITH.
...NOT KNOW-ING...

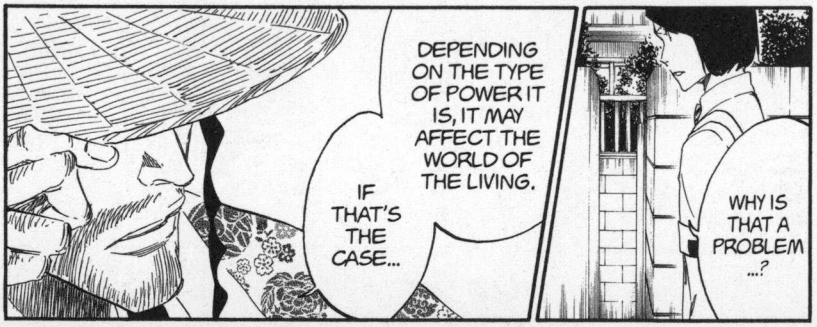
IF THAT'S THE CASE...
DEPENDING ON THE TYPE OF POWER IT IS, IT MAY AFFECT THE WORLD OF THE LIVING.
WHY IS THAT A PROBLEM ...?

...WE CAN'T ALLOW HIM TO COME BACK HERE.
GA
YOU...
...THAT'S HOW IT'LL BE.
IF THAT'S HOW IT IS...
YOU'RE TALKING POSSI-BILITIES ...
AM I RIGHT ?
WELL THAT'S AWFULLY CONVENIENT FOR YOU GUYS, ISN'T IT?!
... AND CLAIMING THAT'S WHAT'S BEST FOR THE WORLD OF THE LIVING!!
KEEPING HIM TRAPPED THERE...

READ THIS WAY
WHAT ARE ...
...THE CHANCES OF IT GOING EXACTLY ...
...AS YOU HYPOTHESIZE?
ONE IN TEN THOUSAND OR...
PERHAPS EVEN LESS.
YOU CAME ALL THE WAY HERE TO TELL US ABOUT SOMETHING THAT'S...
COULD YOU SAY...
I'M SAYING...
... A CHANCE OF IT HAPPENING IS IN THE REALM OF POSSIBILITIES.
THAT'S ALL.
...KEEPING HIS FRIENDS IN THE DARK ABOUT SOMETHING EVEN ON THAT LEVEL ...
...IS DOING RIGHT BY ICHIGO?

BA—M
HERE YOU GO!
AND SO...

WHAT'S THIS...?

UMM...
SHOULDN'T THESE BE...
DON'T WORRY.
I'VE ALREADY SENT SOME TO ICHIGO'S FAMILY.

THOSE ARE CALLED SOUL TICKETS.
IT'S A...
...TRANSIT PERMIT THAT'LL ALLOW YOU TO FREELY ENTER THE SOUL SOCIETY...
...IN CASE ICHIGO WON'T BE ABLE TO LEAVE.

READ THIS WAY
IT'S STILL A WAYS DOWN THE ROAD.
IT'S NOT LIKE IT'S GOING TO BE TODAY OR TOMORROW.
DON'T LOOK SO SAD...
I'LL TELL HIM TO SPEND SOME TIME HERE UNTIL...
...THE BATTLE STARTS.
WHEN ICHIGO EVENTUALLY RETURNS...
...I'LL TELL HIM TO COME BACK HERE.

YOU TIRED, INOUE?
WANNA CALL IT A DAY?

GULP

I WAS JUST...
...THINKING HOW PEACEFUL IT WAS.

NO.
I'M FINE.

YOU KNOW WE'RE TRAINING FOR A BATTLE, RIGHT?
PEACEFUL?
WELL YEAH, BUT...
TMP

I JUST THINK ...
...THAT'S KINDA NICE.
STILL ...
WORKING HARD FOR THE SOUL REAPERS ...
FOR US HUMANS TO BE IN HUECO MUNDO...
HELPING THE ARRAN-CARS...

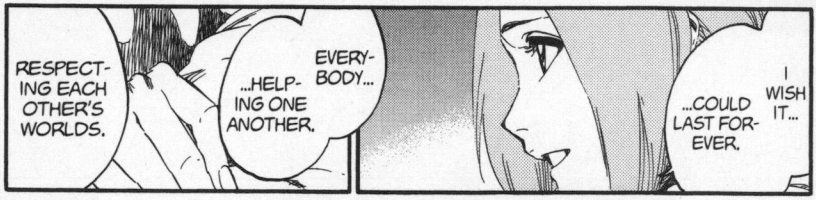
RESPECT-ING EACH OTHER'S WORLDS.
...HELP-ING ONE ANOTHER.
EVERY-BODY...
...COULD LAST FOR-EVER.
I WISH IT...

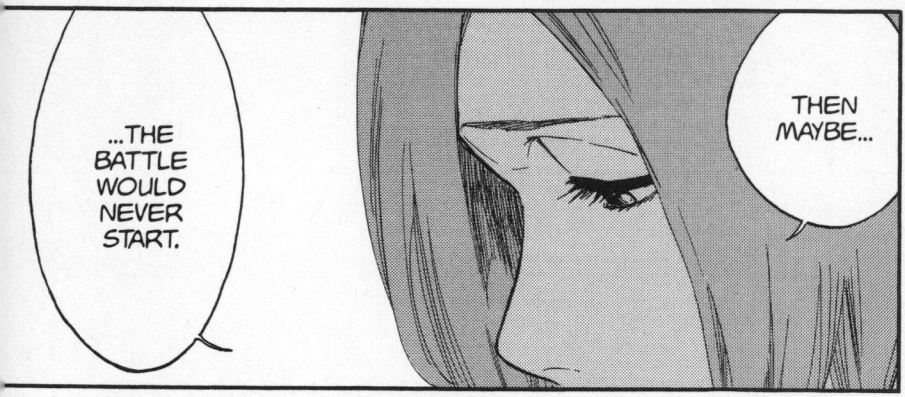
...THE BATTLE WOULD NEVER START.
THEN MAYBE...

WHAT HAPPENED TO THIS PLACE?!
WHAT WAS THAT ...?!
WHAT THE...

THIS ...
THIS CAN'T BE...!!
I DON'T BE-LIEVE THIS...
WHAT'S GOING ON?!!
ALL THE METERS ARE GOING BERSERK !!
...GONE !!!
THE SEIREITEI IS...
...IS COM-PLETE.
THE INVA-SION ...
DO YOU KNOW THE KAISER GESANG? (KING'S HYMN)
URYU.

HIS STRENGTH AFTER 9 YEARS.
HIS MIND AFTER 90 YEARS.
...REGAINS HIS PULSE AFTER 900 YEARS.
THE CONFINED QUINCY KING...
YES.
HIS STRENGTH AFTER 9 YEARS.
HIS MIND AFTER 90 YEARS.
...REGAINS HIS PULSE AFTER 900 YEARS.
THE CONFINED QUINCY KING...
THERE IS MORE TO THE SONG...
AND THE WORLD IN 9 DAYS.

LET US GO.
URYU.
HASCH-WALTH.
BLEACH 546.
THIS IS THE LAST 9 DAYS OF THE WORLD.
THE LAST 9DAYS

547. PEACE FROM SHADOWS
GA
K

BLEACH
ブリーチ

WHAT THE...

BLEACH 547.
Peace from Shadows
THE SEIREI-TEI...
WHAT THE...
...HELL IS HAPPEN-ING!!

WHOO
...DIS-
APPEARING
!!!
SEIREITEI
IS...
WHOOOO

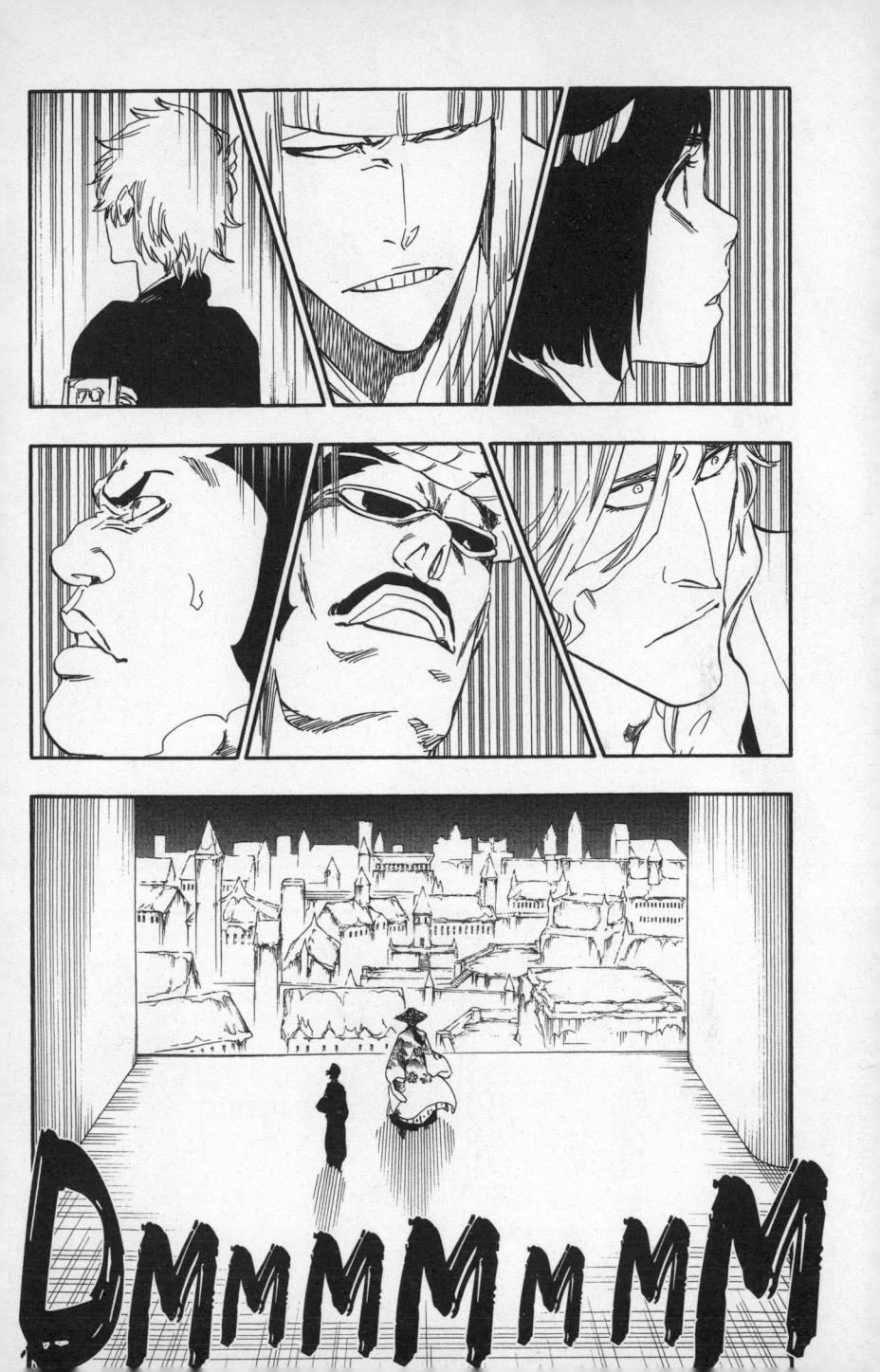
DMMMMMMM

READ THIS WAY
BUT I WASN'T EXPECTING TO LOSE OUR TERRITORIAL ADVANTAGE LIKE THIS...
...EXPECTING THEM TO ATTACK AGAIN WITHOUT WARNING.
OH BOY ...
I SET SOME TRAPS WITHIN SEIREITEI...
RMBLRMBLRMBLRMBLRMBLRMBLRMBL
WOOO
CAPTAIN UKITAKE!!
THE SEIREITEI IS...
CAPTAIN !!
TMP
CAPTAIN !!
AH ...
GASP ...

SHUT UP, AKON!!
HIYOSU.
DAMN IT!!
DAMN IT!
NOTHING'S SHOWING UP ON THE SCREEN!
YOU KNOW BETTER THAN ANYBODY.
THE NUMBERS YOU'RE SEEING ARE EVERY-THING.
ARE YOU DENYING THE INSTRUMENTS WE DEVELOPED OURSELVES?
SEIREITEI IS GONE ?!
YEAH RIGHT!!
THE INSTRUMENTS HERE HAVEN'T DISAPPEARED ...
WHAT ABOUT THE REALITY WE'RE SEEING WITH OUR EYES?!
BAM

ZWO
USR

W...

DAMN IT...!!

WHAT ...
WHAT'S GOING ON...?

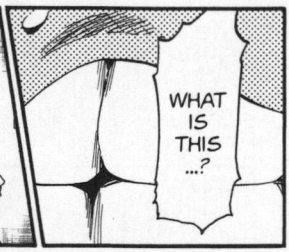
WHAT IS THIS ...?

...THE HELL IS HAPPENING ?!!
YOU WILL NEVER KNOW.
WE QUINCIES LOST THE BATTLE A THOUSAND YEARS AGO AND LEFT WITH NO PLACE TO GO.
SO WE ...
...FLED FROM THE WORLD OF THE LIVING INTO THE SEIREITEI. A PLACE YOU WOULD LEAST EXPECT US TO HIDE.
AND...
...WE CREATED SPACES WITH REISHI INSIDE THE SHADOWS OF THIS WORLD.

...THE VANDENREICH, THE INVISIBLE EMPIRE.
THAT'S WHY WE CALLED IT...

THE THINGS WE COULD DO WITH IT WERE INFINITE.
UNLIKE THE WORLD OF THE LIVING, THE SOUL SOCIETY IS FILLED WITH REISHI, OUR SOURCE OF POWER.
THE PLAN WAS A SUCCESS.

!!

IN OTHER WORDS...
TMP
...BUILDING UP OUR STRENGTH FROM WITHIN THE SHADOWS.
WE SPENT...
...A THOUSAND YEARS...

WE WERE ALREADY HERE TO BEGIN WITH.
TMP
...WE DIDN'T...
...INVADE SEIREITEI BY BREAKING THROUGH THE SHAKONMAKU BARRIER THIS TIME OR THE LAST TIME.

!!

IT DIDN'T TAKE LONG FOR YOU GUYS TO REACH WHERE THE CAPTAIN'S ROOM WAS.
IT SEEMS OUR ENEMY IS BLESSED WITH WELL-TRAINED MEN.
THANKS FOR THE VALUABLE INFORMATION.
HI THERE ...

...JUGRAM HASCHWALTH.
VANDENREICH EMPEROR AIDE AND STERN RITTER GRAND MASTER...

OR DOES THE FACT YOU'RE HERE MEAN YOU KNEW?
I'VE JUST BEEN APPOINTED, SO YOU PROBABLY DIDN'T KNOW THAT...
THIRTEEN COURT GUARD SQUAD CAPTAIN GENERAL AND SQUAD ONE COMPANY CAPTAIN SHUNSUI KYORAKU.

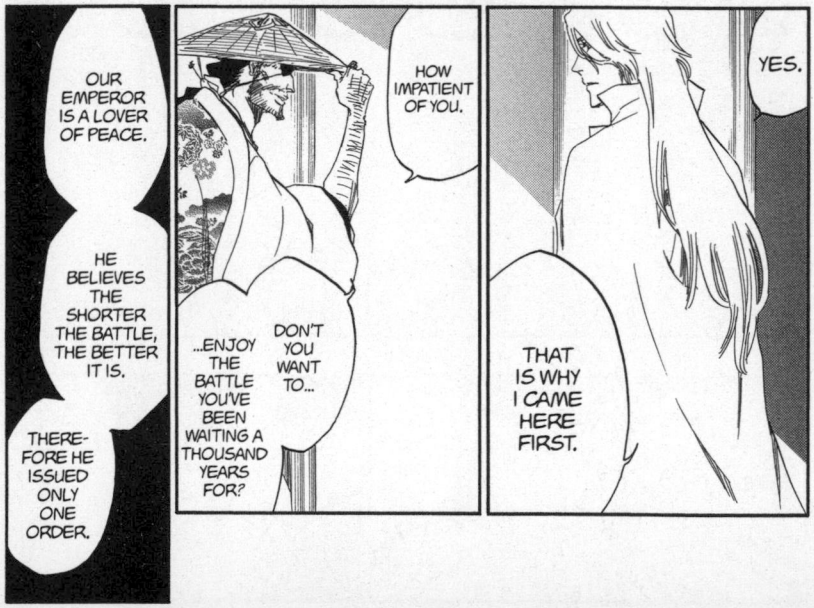
OUR EMPEROR IS A LOVER OF PEACE.
HE BELIEVES THE SHORTER THE BATTLE, THE BETTER IT IS.
THERE-FORE HE ISSUED ONLY ONE ORDER.
...ENJOY THE BATTLE YOU'VE BEEN WAITING A THOUSAND YEARS FOR?
DON'T YOU WANT TO...
HOW IMPATIENT OF YOU.
THAT IS WHY I CAME HERE FIRST.
YES.

I SEE...
"EXTER-MINATE..."
"...THE ENEMY INSTANTLY."

WOOOOOOOO

...DID YOU GET IN HERE?!
HOW THE HELL ...

WHO ARE YOU ...?

WHOA, WHOA, WHOA. DIDN'T YOU LISTEN TO MY EXPLANATION?
OR IS THE RESEARCH AND DEVELOPMENT DEPARTMENT ONLY CLEVER IN NAME?
WE'VE ...
WE DIDN'T GET IN HERE FROM ANYWHERE.
...BEEN HERE FROM THE BEGINNING.

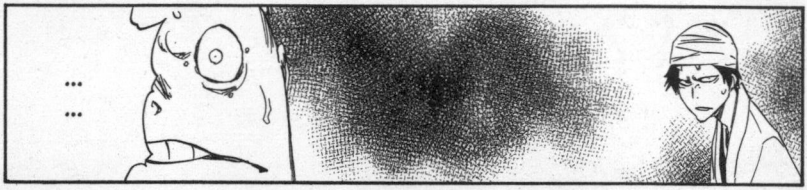
...
...

CLNK...
EXACTLY.

TMTP
HOWEVER...
CREATING ANOTHER WORLD INSIDE THE SHADOWS IS UTTERLY INCONSIDERATE ...
OH MY...
PSsSSSH...
THEY JUST NEVER CAME IN CONTACT WITH ONE ANOTHER.
TWO WORLDS EXISTED SIMULTANEOUSLY IN THE SAME PLACE.
YOU QUINCIES WERE IN THE SHADOWS.

FLAAASH

...IN-CONSIDERATE THINGS.

...I DON'T HATE...

...IF WE ARE ONLY CLEVER IN NAME.
...GO AHEAD AND TRY TO FIND OUT...

DMMMMM

THP

DON'T LET HIM THROUGH !!
DO NOT LET HIM THROUGH !!
D...
DAMN IT...
DANG
KLANGKLANG

HAH!
DO NOT LET ME THROUGH? ARE YOU STUPID?!
THE INVASION'S ALREADY COMPLETE.
SEIREI-TEI'S GONE!
IT'S WAY BEYOND THE POINT OF LETTING US IN OR KEEPING US OUT!
!
YOU MAY BE RIGHT.
IT MAY BE BEYOND LETTING YOU GUYS IN OUR OUT.
HOW-EVER ...

...YOUR FLAME DIDN'T GET THROUGH.

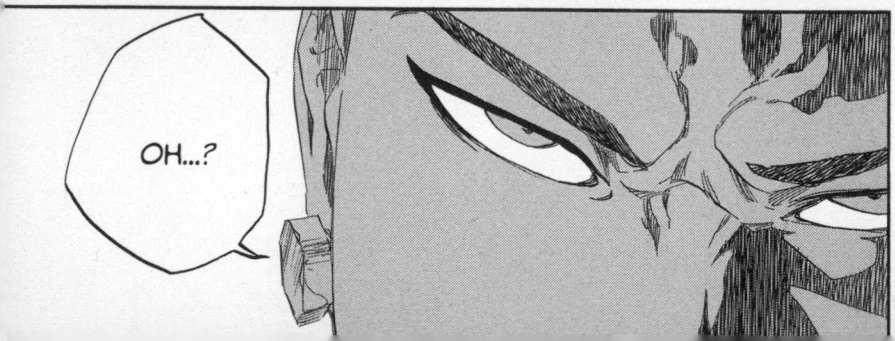
OH...?

548. THE THIN ICE

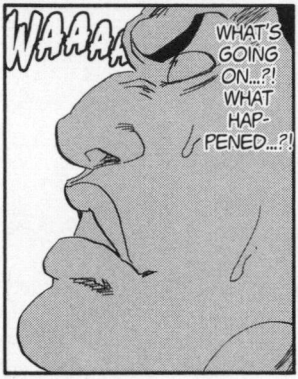

MUST YOU GO...?
BIG BROTH-ER..

PLEASE DO NOT GO...
MAREYO IS FRIGHT-ENED...
JUST PLEASE STAY HERE...
YOU DO NOT HAVE TO PLAY WITH ME ANY-MORE...

I HAVE TO GO.
NO.

YOUR BROTHER IS NOT LEAVING HERE TO SCARE YOU.
MA-REYO.
I KNOW YOU'RE SMART ENOUGH TO UNDER-STAND.

BROTH-ER...

AND...
...THE SEIREITEI.
THAT'S WHY I MUST GO.
OUR NEIGHBOR GONDAWARA AND KANE-MITSU.
...SABURO, OUR SISTER, FATHER, AND MOTHER.
IN ORDER TO PROTECT YOU...

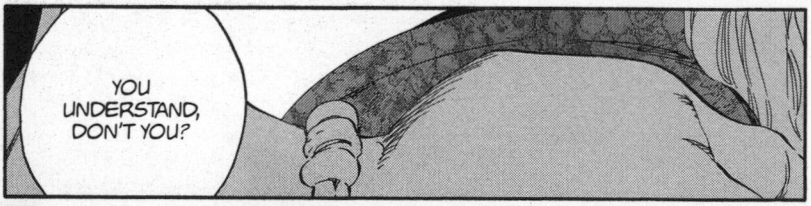
YOU UNDERSTAND, DON'T YOU?

...IS A MEMBER OF THE THIRTEEN COURT GUARD SQUADS.
BECAUSE YOUR BROTHER...

I'LL BE BACK SOON...
SNIFF...
H-HEY! DON'T GIMME THAT LOOK!

GSH
K

KYUU UUU
UUU

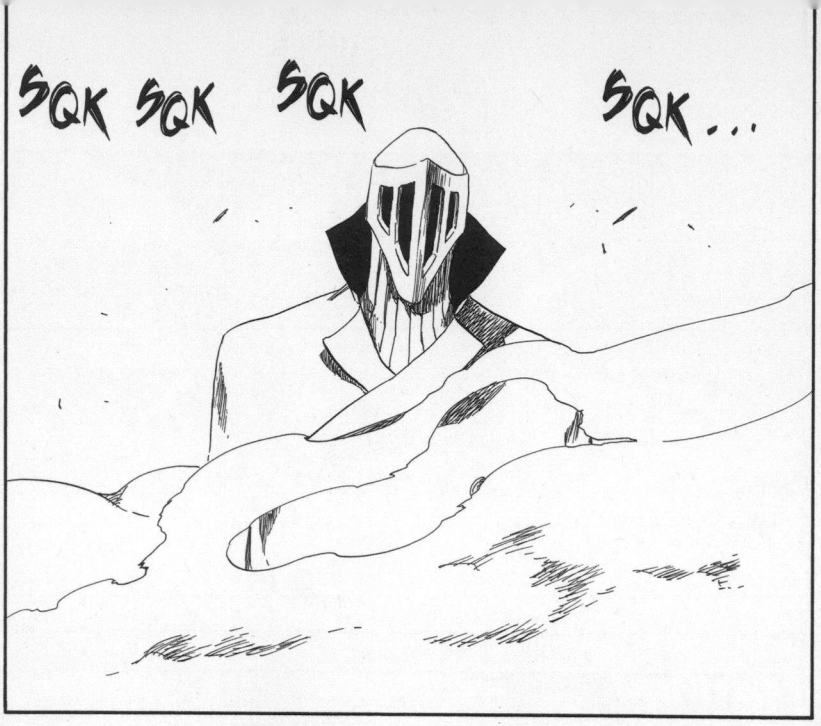
SQK SQK SQK SQK...

...THE GUY WHO STOLE CAPTAIN SOI FON'S BANKAI...
YOU'RE...

BLEACH
548.

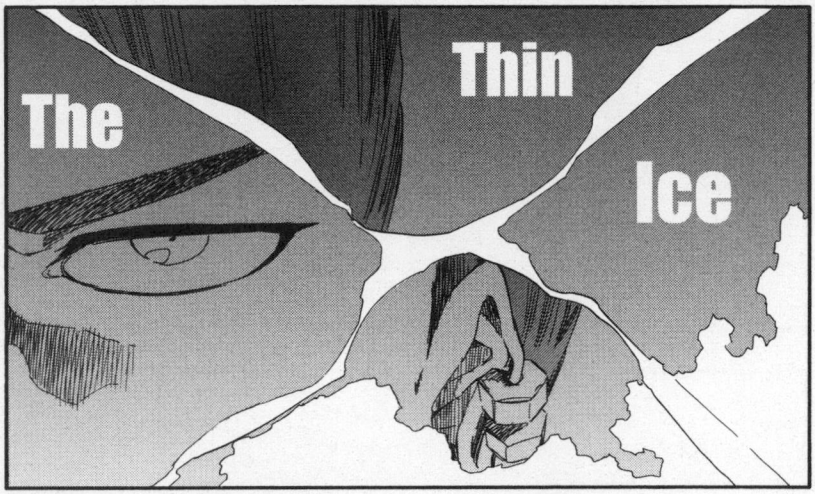
The Thin Ice

RAAAAA!!

LOOK AT WHAT WE HAVE HERE.
I REMEMBER NOW.

YOU'RE CAPTAIN ICE...
...WHO LOST HIS BANKAI TO CANG DU.
KCH
K
SQUAD 10 CAPTAIN TOSHIRO HITSUGAYA.
STERN RITTER "H"!
"THE HEAT"!
WOOF
BAZZ-B!

WHO
SEEMS LIKE WE'RE A GOOD MATCH!
AN AWFUL GOOD MATCH!!
IT SEEMS SO.

DOOO

HEY ...
LOOK AT THIS ICE...
Y...
YES, MA'AM!
WILL HE BE ALL RIGHT ...?!
CAPTAIN HITSU-GAYA...
IT'S A MIRACLE THIS THING SAVED US FROM THAT FIRE...
THE ICE THAT PROTECTED US FROM THAT FLAME... IT'S SO THIN...
HEY, HEY, HEY, HEY!
WELL THIS ICE IS AWFULLY THIN!!
WOOOF

A LITTLE BIT MORE...
...RAISE THE HUMIDITY AROUND HERE!!
SPREAD THAT THING ALL YOU WANT. I'LL MELT IT WITH MY FLAME AND...

LET ME HELP YOU!
THE MEN HAVE ALL FALLEN BACK!
TMP
CAP-TAIN!

WHAT ...?
OH NOTHING! ♪
STARE
IT SEEMS I STILL CAN'T CONTROL IT BY MYSELF.
THANKS.
SORRY.

I WAS JUST THINK-ING...
...LOSING YOUR BANKAI WASN'T ALL BAD.
IT'S SO...
...CUTE THAT YOU'RE RELYING ON ME. ♪
WHAT ...?!
MATSU-MOTO!!
OKAY, OKAY. HERE I GO!
GROWL ...
...HAINEKO!
OPERATION MILLE-FEUILLE !!
I NEVER GAVE IT SUCH A NAME!
WHAT NOW?
SWOOSH

GL
N...
K
SSSSH
FWP
HAI-NEKO!
HOUSE!
HOW'S IT DIFFERENT FROM BEFORE ?!
JUST ANOTHER WALL OF ICE?!
GWF
BO
OF
UMP

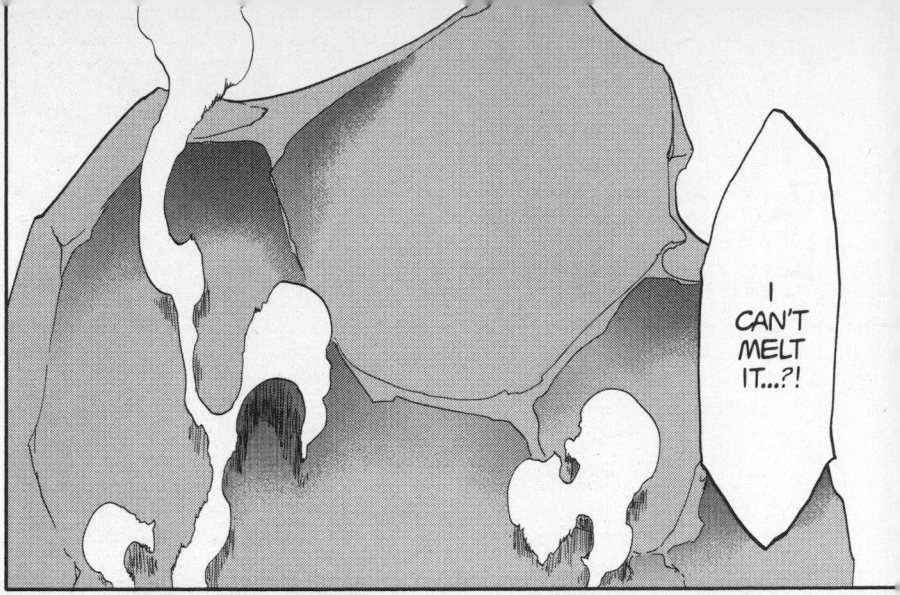
I CAN'T MELT IT...?!

IT'S A MULTI-LAYERED WALL OF VACUUM-ICE.
!

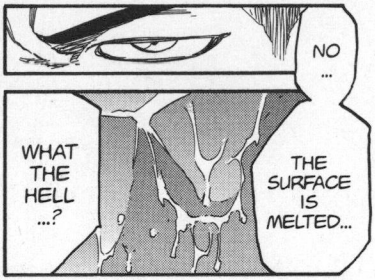
NO ...
THE SURFACE IS MELTED...
WHAT THE HELL ...?

MY HYORINMARU IS PROBABLY THE ZANPAKU-TO...
...WITH THE LEAST AMOUNT OF DIFFERENCE FROM SHIKAI TO BANKAI OUT OF ALL CAPTAINS' SWORDS.

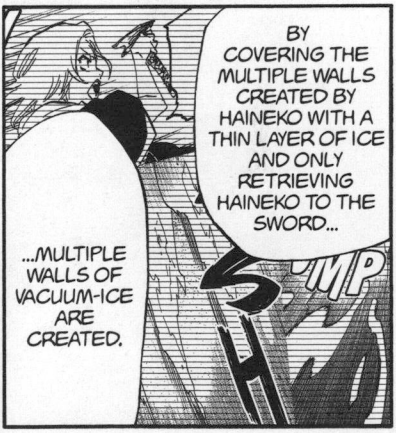
BY COVERING THE MULTIPLE WALLS CREATED BY HAINEKO WITH A THIN LAYER OF ICE AND ONLY RETRIEVING HAINEKO TO THE SWORD...
...MULTIPLE WALLS OF VACUUM-ICE ARE CREATED.
SHIMP

TO MAKE UP FOR IT, I TRAINED MYSELF TO FIGHT WITH LESS ICE.
...THE AMOUNT OF ICE IT CAN CREATE IS SIMPLY DRASTICALLY REDUCED.
THAT'S BECAUSE ...
BUT IT SEEMS IT'S JUST ENOUGH ICE...
...TO BLOCK YOUR FLAME.
YOU BASTARD !!

YOUR FLAME...
...CANNOT PENETRATE THIS WALL OF VACUUM-ICE.

I TOLD YOU IT WON'T GO THROUGH.

GRK...
GRK

NOW...

ZP..
P

BE SHRED-DED...
...BY A BLADE OF ICE.

BIG BROTHER

549. THE STORMBRINGER

BLEACH 549.

The StormBringer

WHERE IS YOUR COMPANY'S CAPTAIN?
THIS IS MY THIRD TIME ASKING.
I AM HOPING FOR AN ANSWER THIS TIME.

I SEARCHED THE AREA USING SPIRITUAL PRESSURE SAMPLES I ACQUIRED DURING OUR LAST BATTLE, BUT I COULD NOT LOCATE YOUR CAPTAIN.
I EVEN EXTENDED THE SEARCH OUTSIDE THE SEIREITEI.
HOW SHOULD I KNOW ...?
SO YOU REFUSE TO ANSWER.

ARE YOU STUPID?! HOW MANY TIMES DO I HAVE TO TELL YOU?!
I REALLY DON'T KNOW!!
USUALLY IN THESE SITUATIONS PEOPLE WON'T TELL YOU EVEN IF THEY DID KNOW TO TRY TO PROTECT WHOEVER IT IS THEY WANNA PROTECT, BUT I SERIOUSLY DON'T KNOW!!
SHE DIDN'T TELL ME!!!
YOU DON'T KNOW MY PERSONALITY, DO YOU?!
IF I'M TOLD ...
...NOT TO GIVE UP THE CAPTAIN'S WHEREABOUTS, I'M THE KINDA GUY WHO'D LET IT SLIP OUT!!

...THE CAPTAIN WOULD NEVER LOSE TO SOMEBODY LIKE YOU ANYWAY!
ALTHOUGH EVEN IF YOU DID FIND OUT...

LET ME ASK YOU ANOTHER WAY.
A THIRD REFUSAL TO ANSWER.

FWK
!

KR
UK
WHAT THE HELL ARE YOU...
KOFF ?!
BIG...
BROTH-ER...
MARE...
...CHIYO...

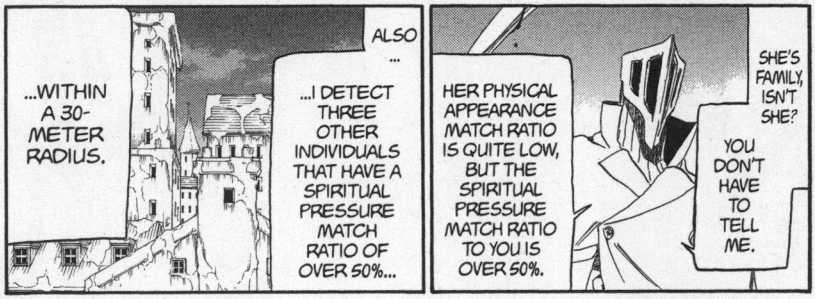
...WITHIN A 30-METER RADIUS.
ALSO ...
...I DETECT THREE OTHER INDIVIDUALS THAT HAVE A SPIRITUAL PRESSURE MATCH RATIO OF OVER 50%...
HER PHYSICAL APPEARANCE MATCH RATIO IS QUITE LOW, BUT THE SPIRITUAL PRESSURE MATCH RATIO TO YOU IS OVER 50%.
SHE'S FAMILY, ISN'T SHE?
YOU DON'T HAVE TO TELL ME.

...WILL DIE THE EXACT MOMENT OF YOUR NEXT REFUSAL TO ANSWER.
ALL OF THEM...

GA DON

LET MAREYO GO!!
KTNK
CAN I...
...TAKE THIS AS A REFUSAL TO ANSWER?
I HAVE TWO QUES-TIONS...
IF I LET HER GO NOW...
...SHE WILL LOSE A LARGE VOLUME OF BODILY FLUIDS AND DIE.
ARE YOU FINE WITH THAT?
SHK SHK SHK

CLNG
CLNG
CLNG
NO
SH
K
I'M HOPING FOR AN ANSWER.
THERE IS A POSSIBILITY YOU LOST YOUR FUNCTION OF SPEECH FROM SHOCK.
I WILL GIVE YOU A 15-SECOND REPRIEVE.
YOU'RE DEAD ...
KOFF...
YOU ARE DEAD ...
YOUR 15 SECONDS ARE UP.
I'M GONNA MAKE YOU PAY FOR THIS!!!

GCH
K
HOW UN-FORTUNATE.
YOU BASTAAAARD !!!
KAKAK
KAKAK

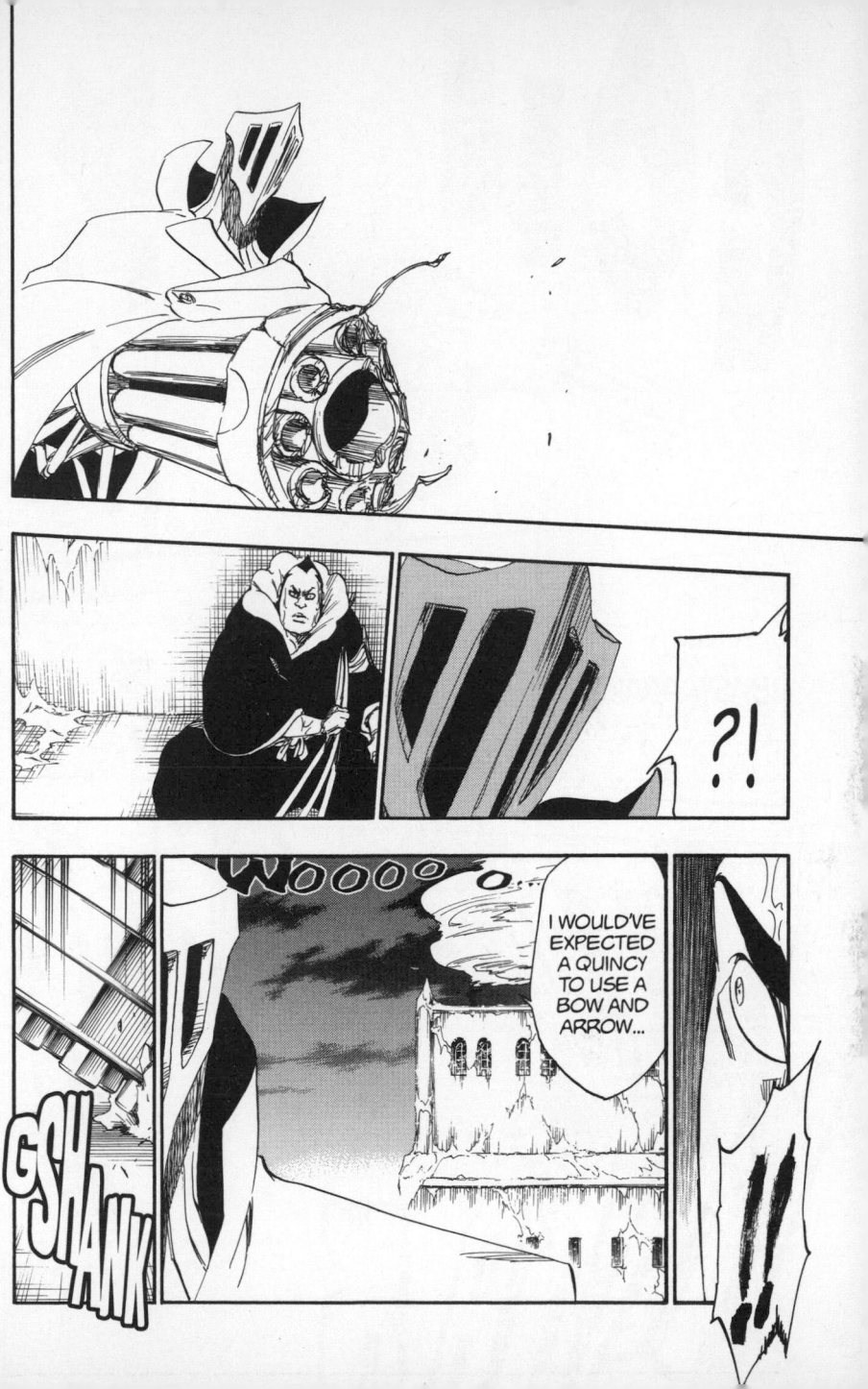
?!
WOOOO
I WOULD'VE EXPECTED A QUINCY TO USE A BOW AND ARROW...
GSHANK
!!

YOU'RE A LOT MORE SOPHISTICATED THAN I HAD HEARD.

IT'S SHUNKO.

DID YOU THINK I WOULD LET IT STAY UNPER-FECTED?

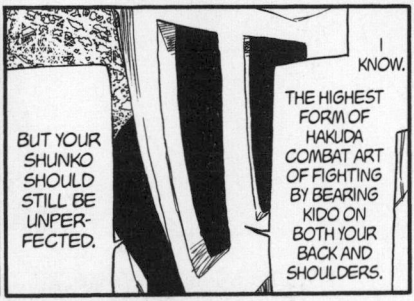
I KNOW.
THE HIGHEST FORM OF HAKUDA COMBAT ART OF FIGHTING BY BEARING KIDO ON BOTH YOUR BACK AND SHOULDERS.
BUT YOUR SHUNKO SHOULD STILL BE UNPER-FECTED.

AND UNTIL TODAY, I HAVE BEEN TRAINING TO IMPROVE IT EVEN FURTHER.

I PERFECTED SHUNKO AFTER MY BATTLE WITH YORUICHI.

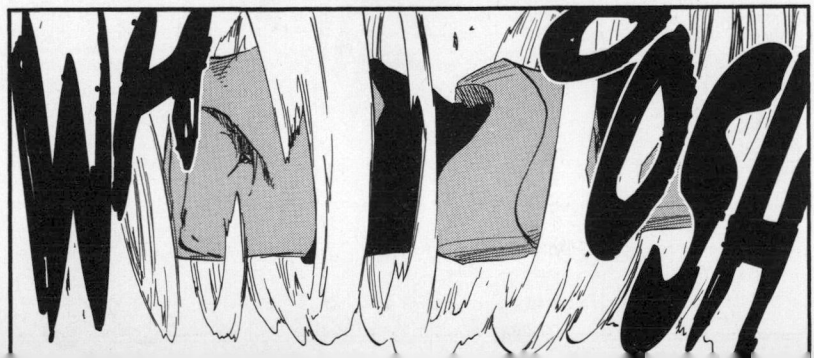
WHI
OSH

WHOOF
WHOO
I THANK YOU.
IF I HADN'T LOST MY BANKAI TO YOU, I MAY NOT HAVE BEEN ABLE TO IMPROVE SHUNKO THIS MUCH.
...IT HAS BEEN ACTIVATED, I CAN KEEP FIGHTING WHILE DONNING SHUNKO.
AND ONCE ...
I DISCOVERED A WAY TO WRAP MY BODY WITH A VORTEX OF SPIRITUAL PRESSURE.
MY SHUNKO IS WIND.
WHOO...OO

MUKYU SHUNKO! (INFINITE SHUNKO)

GWOOO
SH
GASP!
THIS SPIRITUAL PRESSURE IS...!!
RMBL
RMBL RMBL RMBL
CAPTAIN SOI FON DID IT TOO!!
IT'S CAPTAIN SOI FON!!
DADOO OOM

!
RMBL
RMRIP
BUT ...
MAY-BE...
SHALL WE GO HELP THE OTHER CAPTAINS ?
THINGS ARE LOOKING UP, CAP-TAIN.

HEY, HEY, HEY ...
C'MON, MAN.

ZLCH
YOU GONNA LEAVE ME HANGING HERE WHILE WE'RE STILL WARMING UP?

...BEGUN FIGHTING YET!
I HAVEN'T EVEN...
HA HA HA
...K
KN
WM

MMM...
MM...

NOT HAPPENING!

I'M GONNA PASS.
I GET THE FEELING YOU'LL TAKE TOO LONG.

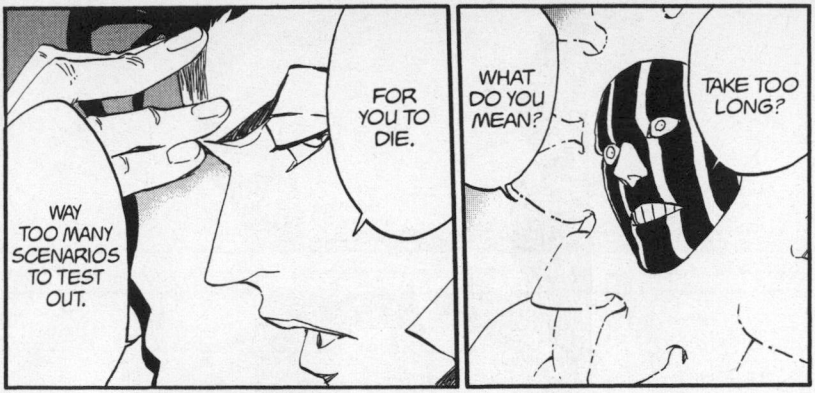
WAY TOO MANY SCENARIOS TO TEST OUT.
FOR YOU TO DIE.
WHAT DO YOU MEAN?
TAKE TOO LONG?

GOOD-BYE.
YOU SHOULD GO FIND SOME-BODY ELSE TO FIGHT.
I LIKE TO ZIP RIGHT THROUGH IT.
I...
...REALLY HATE THOSE KINDS OF LITTLE THINGS.

GO WHER-EVER YOU PLEASE.
NO.
AREN'T YOU GOING TO STOP ME...?

TMP
TMP
TMP

TMP...

OR WHAT?
I WOULD LIKE SOME TIME MYSELF TO ANALYZE YOUR SPIRITUAL PRESSURE.

I'M GLAD I DIDN'T CARELESSLY SHOW YOU MY ABILITY.
HOW SCARY ...

... STEP INTO YOUR TERRITORY?
WERE YOU TRYING TO GET ME TO...

ZOM...
!
M

I KNEW IT...

IT SEEMS SHE DEFEATED THE ENEMY WITHOUT HAVING BANKAI!
IT SEEMS SO!
RMBL RMBL
SO! FON.
THIS SPIRITUAL PRESSURE IS...

JUST AS HIS MAJESTY PREDICTED.
...WILL LEARN HOW TO FIGHT WITHOUT IT IN A SHORT PERIOD OF TIME.
THE CAPTAINS WHO LOST THEIR BANKAI ...

IF IT WAS PRE-DICTED...
I KNOW YOU...
...KNOW WHAT THAT MEANS.

...IT MEANS THE SITUATION ...
...IS STILL CRITICAL FOR YOUR SIDE.

BLEACH 550.

Blazing Bullets
UHDOOOM
GSHK
SPLCH
KLKL
UK
K

D
M
M

HE SHOULDA BEEN RIPPED APART BY CAPTAIN HITSU-GAYA'S ICE...
N...
HE... NO WAY...

GCHK
LOOK.
MY BEST STERN RITTER UNIFORM IS RUINED.
I WAS RIPPED APART.
AT LEAST MY CAPE WAS.

FWAA
P

WHOOSH
GA K
SHH
HP
BOOF

WHAT A MON-STER.
TMP
YOU'RE STILL BREATH-ING...?

GKAKAKA
GRUK

KLUK
LUK

PSHHH

SOME-THING KURO-TSUCHI WOULD ENJOY.
A MECH-ANICAL DOLL, HUH?

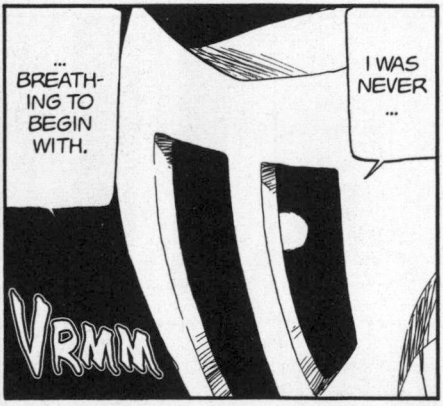
... BREATH-ING TO BEGIN WITH.
I WAS NEVER ...
VRMM

SCHK

MUKYU SHUNKO.
I HAVE RECEIVED VERY USEFUL DATA.
HOW-EVER..

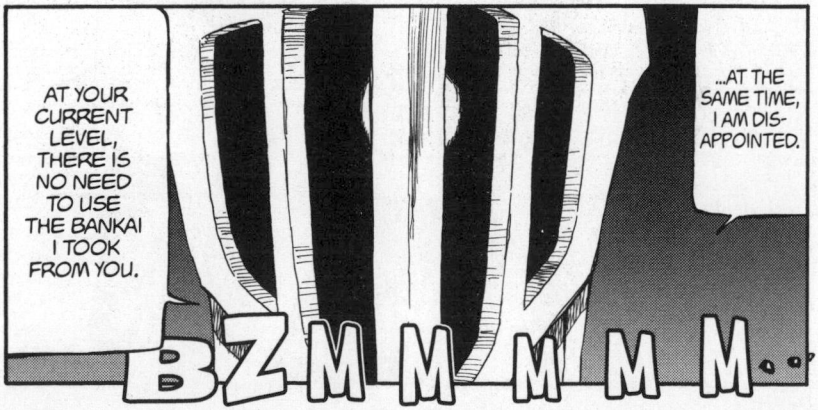
...AT THE SAME TIME, I AM DIS-APPOINTED.
AT YOUR CURRENT LEVEL, THERE IS NO NEED TO USE THE BANKAI I TOOK FROM YOU.
BZMMMMM...

DMM DMM DMM
C...
CAP-TAIN !!
BUSH
DID YOU REALLY THINK...
...YOU COULD TAKE ME OUT WITH THIS?!
THINK AGAIN!

I TOLD YOU.
!!!
I HAVE RECEIVED...
...USEFUL DATA ON MUKYU SHUNKO.
DAMN IT...
BZ
MM...M

BOOM

LET ME TELL YOU SOMETHING.
YOU SAID YOU COULD SHIELD MY FLAME EARLIER.

SO WHY DO YOU THINK WE'RE STILL ALIVE?
HE DIDN'T MISS.
WE WERE ALL DIRECTLY STRUCK BY IT.
!
THE STERN RITTERS WHO WERE BURNED BY YOUR CAPTAIN GENERAL...
...ARE ALL ALIVE.
INCLUDING ME.

I CANCELED OUT...
...YOUR CAPTAIN GENERAL'S FLAMES WITH MINE!

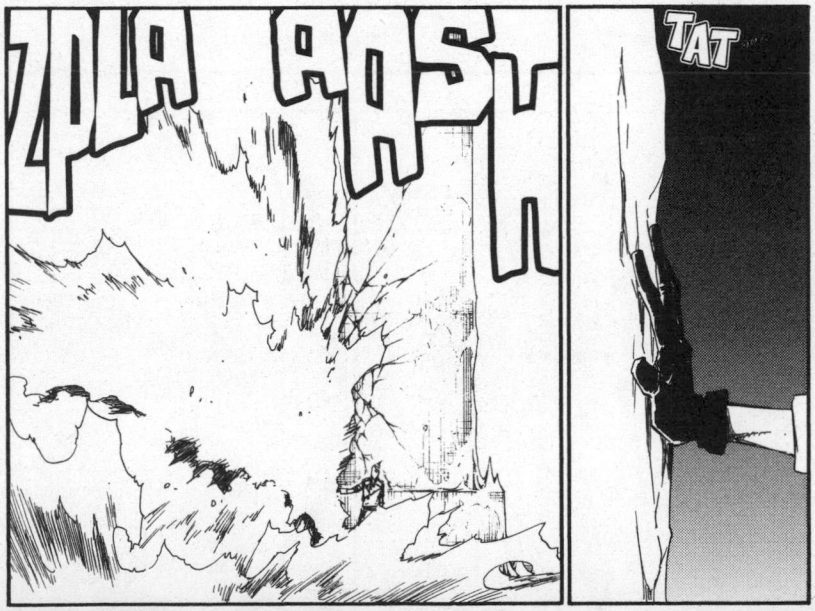
ZPLA
ASH
TAT

...THAT I ONLY NEED A FINGER TO FIGHT AGAINST YOUR ICE.
I COULD'VE SHOWN YOU...
IT'S TOO BAD YOU DON'T HAVE BANKAI RIGHT NOW.
GWOOF
SPLAASH

IT WON'T REACH ME.
YES, SIR!
MATSUMOTO, FALL BACK! WE NEED TO REGROUP!!
I'LL DELAY HIM WITH MY RYOJIN HYOHEKI ICE WALL!

...BUT ALL I NEED IS A FINGER.
BUT I'LL TELL YOU THIS.
YOU CAN TRY WHAT-EVER YOU WANT WITH YOUR ICE...
A WALL OF FINELY WOVEN ICE.
YOU GOT A LOT UP YOUR SLEEVES.
ZSHAAA

ONE!
BURNER FINGER...

CONTI
NUED
IN
BLEACH
62

DISCOVER ANIME
IN A WHOLE NEW WAY!

www.neonalley.com

What it is...

- Streaming anime delivered 24/7 straight to your TV via your connected video game console
- All English dubbed content
- Anime, martial arts movies, and more

Go to **neonalley.com** for news, updates and to see if Neon Alley is available in your area.

NEON ALLEY is a trademark or service mark of VIZ Media, LLC

P9-DDM-525

You're Reading in the Wrong Direction!!

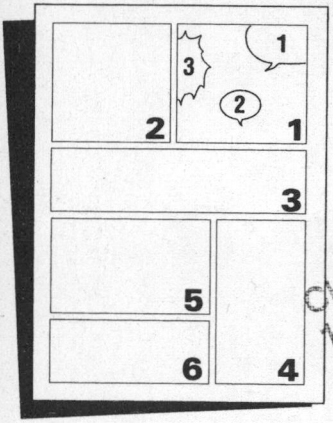

Whoops! Guess what? You're starting at the wrong end of the comic!

...It's true! In keeping with the original Japanese format, **Bleach** is meant to be read from right to left, starting in the upper-right corner.

Unlike English, which is read from left to right, Japanese is read from right to left, meaning that action, sound effects and word-balloon order are completely reversed... something which can make readers unfamiliar with Japanese feel pretty backwards themselves. For this reason, manga or Japanese comics published in the U.S. in English have sometimes been published "flopped"—that is, printed in exact reverse order, as though seen from the other side of a mirror.

By flopping pages, U.S. publishers can avoid confusing readers, but the compromise is not without its downside. For one thing, a character in a flopped manga series who once wore in the original Japanese version a T-shirt emblazoned with "M A Y" (as in "the merry month of") now wears one which reads "Y A M"! Additionally, many manga creators in Japan are themselves unhappy with the process, as some feel the mirror-imaging of their art skews their original intentions.

We are proud to bring you Tite Kubo's **Bleach** in the original unflopped format. For now, though, turn to the other side of the book and let the adventure begin...!

—Editor

JAN 18
CH